All about
Obedience Training

Also in the 'All About . . .' Series

All about Obedience Training

for Dogs

MOLLIE MULVANY

PELHAM BOOKS

First published in Great Britain by
PELHAM BOOKS
44 Bedford Square, London, WC1B 3DP
FEBRUARY 1973
SECOND EDITION 1978
THIRD EDITION 1986
REPRINTED 1986

British Library Cataloguing in Publication Data

Mulvany, Mollie
   All about obedience. — 3rd ed.
   1. Dogs — Training
   I. Title
   636.7'083   SF431
   ISBN 0-7207-1673-X

Filmset and printed in Great Britain by
BAS Printers Limited, Over Wallop, Hampshire
and bound by Dorstel Press Limited, Harlow

To Fern, Danny, Barry, Dusky, Mandy, Flick and all those great dogs of the past

Contents

ACKNOWLEDGEMENTS

To my husband Peter, and my sister Audrey, for their unstinting help and encouragement at all times. All knowledge is acquired somewhere and I am deeply indebted to literally hundreds of people in dog training whose interest and discussions have inspired this book and provided me with endless fields to explore.

The photographs appear by kind permission of Cooke (10), Eric Newman (3), Eric Purchase (4–9), C. P. Smith A.I.S.T. (1, 11–19).

Illustrations

Photographs

Line Drawings

1 The Two-Way Contract

Responsibilities of Ownership: Approach to Training:
Avoiding Unpleasantness

Successful dog training is a complex, many-sided affair. Like a number of other worth-while things in life, it offers something for everyone, but the more deeply it is studied, the more time and effort put into its practice, the greater its rewards.

Clearly it is the duty of any responsible dog owner to ensure that adequate training is given to his dog, not only for its own safety and welfare, but for the good of those who come into contact with it. Each dog is an ambassador for all dogs. By its deeds, its character and its behaviour, dogdom is judged. If your dog makes himself a nuisance, jumping up with muddy paws, incessant barking, pushing his way through doors, fouling footpaths, chasing motor vehicles and livestock and, perhaps, perish the thought! even savaging children, he gives fuel to the fire of the anti-dog brigade.

A well-behaved dog, on the other hand, is a happy and pleasant companion to his owner and creates a good impression wherever he goes. It is, therefore, our responsibility as dog-owners to do everything in our power towards making our own dogs good citi   and not confounded nuisances to everyone around.

Training is an absorbing, addictive hobby, and many who read this book will, I hope, become sufficiently involved in teaching good general behaviour that they will want to savour the sweets and satisfactions of competitive work, a fast-growing pastime.

Whatever your aims and ambitions, whether a modest general control over your dog and a commendable desire to mould him into a good companion, or the ultimate in competitive work, I sincerely hope you will find something to help   guide you in these pages. I should, however, make it perfectly clear at the outset that although this book is entitled *All about Obedience Training for Dogs*, no one knows everything there is to know about the subject. When we feel we know it all, we stop learning, and to stop learning means dropping back. Another disillusionment which should come early on is that I shall not be having a magic wand to make you top trainers with brilliant workers! There is no mystic secret, the knowledge of which will turn your dog into an obedience champion. There is nothing you can read here (or anywhere else for that matter) that will even begin to help you if you are not prepared to make your own contribution as well. There are, however, some time and temper savers I hope to tell you about, and there are certain ways of doing things that make training a pleasure for you and learning fun for your dog. I aim to make you more aware of the range of opportunities in training but, without your co-operation, I cannot inject you with knowledge. You must absorb it for yourself and then work at achieving that essential rapport which exists between the successful trainer and his dog.

I shall be telling you all about the many aspects of dog training. I will guide you along a sound basic grounding and explain how I train my own dogs and how I would tackle certain problems, but the ultimate result of what this book means to you and how it helps you is up to you yourself. If I could wave that magic wand, the first person I would wave it over is myself! As it is, I shall continue like everyone else and go along the more usual lines of working actively towards achieving my ambitions, and not simply sit passively whilst some wonderful transformation takes place without my having to make any effort.

'Training is cruel', it is sometimes said. In actual fact, it is far more unkind to neglect a dog's education. It is my opinion that the trained dog is the only truly happy one. He does not necessarily have to be trained up to a very high standard, but he should be guided in such a way that he is able to fit in cheerfully with our way of life, trained by someone who thinks enough of him to take the trouble to help him become a good companion who can go anywhere.

A dog that behaves itself has a greater chance of a happy, decent life than one that doesn't, but, like children, left to their own devices, dogs acquire habits that are not acceptable. It is up to us as responsible owners to help them along the right lines, and that is what this book is all about. For those of you who want to go into more advanced competition work, I hope to include something worth while for you as well.

Methods of training vary, of course, but most modern dog training is considerably less violent than that of the past, for most people nowadays are repulsed and angered by cruelty, whether it is to children, old people or animals. There are, alas, far too many cases even today of deliberate cruelty, as a glance through the records will show. It is a sad reflection on our sense of values that animal life is still held too cheaply, as the disgustingly high numbers of pets destroyed or abandoned at holiday and licensing times reveal.

Although most people of intelligence and sensibility abhor deliberate cruelty, many owners cause their dogs distress through ignorance, and thoughtlessness in training can quickly deteriorate into a form of mental anguish to a dog. There are a number of sources where one can acquire unfortunate 'knowledge' of training. It is bad enough when one's 'amateur' friends advise one to rub a puppy's nose in the mess it has just made or to beat it for crying in the night, but the other day I read a professional 'expert' advising that the way to train a puppy not to jump out of a car until it was told was to slam the door shut in its face. In actual fact, all this will teach the puppy, always supposing of course that you still have a puppy after risking maiming it like this, is to be terrified of cars and of you.

One unkind old-fashioned method of training is that of tempting a dog to 'riot' (i.e. to misbehave and have the fault corrected). A little of this has to be done with gundogs who must know once and for all that fur-chasing is out, and, this is indeed one of the methods suitable for curing a real 'criminal' dog – one that chases and kills livestock, for instance, or that appalling menace to human life, the car-chaser. However, there is no excuse whatsoever for using it in puppy training or in competitive obedience work. In my opinion it is both stupid and callous to invite someone to deliberately try to get a partly-trained dog to make a mistake just so that the handler can come back and reprimand it for not doing as it was told in the first place. There are several similar senseless pieces of advice offered to owners of dogs by those who know nothing better than resorting to unkindness in one degree or another. Obviously there must be discipline and firmness in training. We cannot accept whatever incon-venient behaviour is offered, but there is a world of difference between a cheerful determination to get one's own way with a dog and physical violence or mental torment.

My own method of training has been referred to as a lazy one, partly because I firmly believe the place to train a dog for the most part is at home – preferably in front of the fire watching television – and partly because I am a great believer that in dog training prevention is better than cure. If a young dog is never allowed to do irritating things in the first place or they are quietly nipped in the bud when he first tries them, he does not acquire annoying habits. This may seem a negative type of training but it doesn't really work out that way. What it means is that instead of constant correction for faults the dog has been allowed to acquire in the past, he behaves automatically in a way that fits in with his owner's arrangements because he has never done otherwise. This is the background the dog knows and understands, he has been brought up this way and never considers an alternative. The beauty of all this is that when you start more positive training for competition work, a pleasant relationship has been built up between owner and dog – the dog does nothing to annoy the handler and therefore there is no need for the handler to be constantly correcting him, so they start off in a good attitude of mind to learn together.

This negative early training goes a step further in the use of negative words. 'No' is one of the very first a puppy should learn, the first being its name and 'Come', closely followed by 'Good boy'. 'No', 'Leave' and a very useful disapproving sound, 'Aaah', are extremely important parts of his early vocabulary. Obviously tone of voice is of the utmost importance and you will have to practise giving all the nice words a pleasant, gay tone and all the 'No' words a disapproving tone.

Many dogs are allowed to get out of hand and acquire bad habits *before* their owners contemplate training, and in these cases, of course, preventive training is useless and corrective training must take place. Personally, however, I don't want arguments with my dog. To succeed I know I must win the argument and, depending on how strong willed the dog and how long he has been allowed to get away with something, so depends the strength and possibly the unpleasantness of the argument. How much nicer not to have these arguments in the first place.

Puppies, like very small children, are not filled with evil intentions or deliberate disobedience. These are learned later, helped unwittingly by their owners or, in the case of children, by their parents.

A puppy that jumps up at his owner is doing so because he loves him and is wanting to show that affection in the only way he knows. Whilst most people think there is something lovable (and indeed there is) about this show of affection from a small creature, the same people get very annoyed indeed when the puppy reaches maturity and does the same thing, especially if he has just been for a country walk on a wet day. It is quite illogical to expect a dog to understand why one day his advances are appreciated and the next he is shouted at and even punished for doing what to him is the identical action. He cannot be expected to realise that at times his paws leave stains and at others they do not.

There are times when even a fully trained dog has to be corrected or even punished, but not until other methods have been tried and failed. When a dog that has been acquired at puppyhood needs the maximum correction it is a reflection on the owner who has failed in his responsibility to the dog. Exactly like children, dogs need to understand fully what is required of them to fit in comfortably with society.

You will see, therefore, how important in successful training it is to put into practice the maxim that prevention is better than cure. If you do not allow your dog to make mistakes you do not have to correct him, and everyone is happy.

From time to time I shall refer to what I call 'The Golden Rules of Dog Training', and the first is *Prevention is Better than Cure.*

The second is: *Know Your Dog.* Each dog is an individual. His character, his temperament and his potential are quite different from any other dog you will ever know, so study him closely, find out what makes him tick. Get on the same wavelength as him. If you have a nervous dog, try and discover what has made him nervous. Is it his breeding that has influenced him, or, far more likely, is it environment and upbringing? What has happened to set up the chain of reactions that you now put down to poor temperament – the easy way out which throws all the blame on the breeder and none on you?

He doesn't like children? Trace back to see at what point he decided he didn't like them. You will probably find that he has had a fright from one, or else he played rather too vigorously with one and was harshly treated for it. Perhaps he is nervous of traffic or meeting other dogs. Whatever the type of his nervousness, seek out the cause and tackle his particular problem with patience and understanding.

All dog ownership is a partnership. Dog training takes that partnership several stages further. To be successful both partners must contribute to it, but remember you are the senior partner and must take 75 per cent of the responsibility. To a great extent your dog will become what you make him. By sympathetic handling and skilful guidance of his natural abilities you can do much to make him go the way you want.

There must be a two-way contract between you and your dog. Don't expect the dog to give all with nothing in return. There must be a mutual respect and a mutual trust. Don't bore him. Don't nag him. Don't weary him when he is not feeling 100 per cent. Don't begrudge him his privacy and off time. Make yourself as attractive as you can to your dog. Make sure he feels delighted when you take notice of him and eager to welcome your attention at all times. Of course you will want to look after his physical welfare, and more of that later, but don't neglect his mental well-being, which is so very important. Remember that however much a dog enjoys the company of other dogs, he prefers human companionship every time. Originally he left the pack to be with man, and his greatest ambition is to be the loved and valued companion of his master. Cash in on this avid desire for your company and create a sense of togetherness with the dog which will be his greatest reward.

Have you ever wondered what your dog thinks of you, or do you just take it for granted that because you own him and provide the board and lodging you have his affection and his respect? Some people might have a jolt if they knew what their pets really thought of them! For it makes little difference to your dog how the rest of the world rates you. You can be a hardened criminal or a saint, good looking or ugly, a wealthy man or a poor, a success in life or an abject failure. All your dog will go on is your attitude towards him. Do you trust him as a friend, give him love and care? Do you respect him? If the answer to all these questions is 'Yes', you have every reason to believe that he will return your friendship, your love and care and your respect a hundred times over. Because he thinks so highly of you, your dog will try his best to do what pleases you and will take his cue on behaviour from you.

If you are a moody sort of individual then you will produce a quiet, unsure dog, lacking in confidence when confidence means so much, indecisive as to which course he should take in case he makes the wrong choice. If you are unfair to him in your moodiness you will produce a halting, hesitant dog, one whose defensive action could turn to viciousness and who will invariably work with ears well back.

The most exuberant dogs have the most exuberant handlers. Perhaps these people do not appear particularly exuberant to the rest of us but in the secret corners of their heart they have a yearning to be carefree extroverts. A dog cannot be deceived, and he will zestfully acknowledge this hidden trait. A smiling face which hides a venomous heart dispirits a dog and takes away his joy of life. You cannot deceive him and you cannot deceive anyone who can read a dog, either.

How is it that some people feed and pamper their pets, give them everything they can imagine they wish for and receive a minimum of devotion and yet others who appear rough and ready towards their dogs, hard in training, hard in handling, can arouse a fierce love in the dog who would cheerfully lay his life down for what might seem to the rest of us a very unworthy owner? The way to a dog's heart lies not through its stomach or the luxuries of life, for a dog, as we humans are painfully slow to learn, is incorruptible. He will accept food if he is greedy or if he is hungry, but he does not know the meaning of bribery, hints, promises of better times coming or any of these essentially human 'carrots for the donkey'. Like the donkey himself, the dog sees only the carrot. He does not understand any of the implications behind it. This is one good reason why the habit of bribing a dog with a titbit is futile. It can never achieve the desired result. If the dog performs an exercise correctly it is because he has been taught the exercise correctly. Not because he thinks to himself, 'Now I must get this right because then I'll get a biscuit.'

It would, however, be a pity to conclude from this that dogs do not reason. I am sure that they do, but the difficulty is that we tend to assume they think our way. Again, I am sure they do not. Man likes to think his reason rules his instinct, and to a great extent he is right. The lower down the animal scale we go, the more influence instinct has and the less reason comes into it. However, the dog has been with man for many thousands of years and is in the peculiar position of (1) already being one of the higher/middle animals anyway and therefore balancing his reason/instinct more satisfactorily than most, and (2) being influenced greatly by man to develop his reason and submerge his instincts. We therefore have an animal which is making gallant attempts to understand us, but should not be penalised when we ourselves fail to make our meanings clear enough.

A dog is still far more dominated by instinct and his senses than we often appreciate, and we make training very much more difficult for the dog when we simply assume he thinks and feels about things as we do.

Anyone who has attempted a foreign language will know that repetition with constant practice until the words and phrases become cosily familiar is the most satisfactory and reliable method of learning. The dog is learning a foreign language when we train him, and repetition to form good habits is the most reliable method to use.

Unlike man, however, the dog does not see the reason behind the learning, and it is grossly unfair, therefore, to expect him to concentrate for long stretches of time. A few minutes' training daily, or twice, or even three times daily, are of far greater value than half an hour in any one session.

I hope I have already convinced you that to own a dog is not enough. To reap the rewards of companionship and devotion which any dog, given the opportunity, dedicates to the human race, it is necessary to understand a little of the workings of the dog's mind, and to be prepared to spend some time in trying to appreciate what life means from a dog's eye view.

Taken at its most literal, a dog's eye view is a world of human legs and feet, nylon stockings and slacks, wellington boots and fluffy slippers, table and chair legs, limitless horizons in the open countryside, highly limited horizons in buildings and built-up areas.

Many would have us believe that the dog's view is a colourless one, and certainly it is clear that he does not see things in exactly the same way as we do. From a life-time of the study of dogs, I am convinced that a dog's vision is two-dimensional – that is to say the dog sees things flat and not rounded as his three-dimensional-eyed human counterpart.

If this is indeed true, you will readily appreciate the extraordinary circumstances where an intelligent, trained dog will stare straight through his motionless owner at times (particularly in the early hours before the sun is up and again in the gathering dusk), worried because he has caught the scent but cannot focus you against the background *until you move*. Then, with a joyous bound, he greets you as only a well-loved dog knows how. Again and again in competitive work one sees a dog miss an obvious (to us) retrieve article and find it eventually by scent, and what of the dog of apparently perfect sight who nearly stumbles over motionless game in an away wind, yet can spot a fleeing hare four or five hundred yards away in the same wind conditions?

A favourite theory of mine is that colours to the dog are represented by scents, each colour, e.g. red, having its own scent distinct from say blue or yellow. This again would account for some behaviour of the dog in scent work and it is worth trying various experiments with your dog's ability to colour match. Give him scent with a sterile cloth of a certain colour, then see if he will pick out that colour from a mixture of different coloured cloths. This knack of matching up unscented coloured cloths in many trained dogs tell me (1) that either the dog must be able to distinguish colour and/or (2) that different colours have different scents.

All this leads up to the interesting fact that the dog's vision is largely over-shadowed by that greater sense of his, scent. It is difficult for us to appreciate at times how important to the dog is his nose. It means so much that even if his eyesight fails completely, kept in familiar surroundings and not suddenly subjected to the anxieties of the unknown, the blind dog, helped by an understanding owner, can lead a happy if necessarily limited life. As a blind man finds solace in his brain and intellectual pursuits, so the dog finds his in his extraordinary sense of smell. Perhaps because the dog asks far less of life than man, he can be almost completely happy in these circumstances, whereas the blind man, content though he may be, lacks so much of life when he loses his sight that it would be presumptuous of any sighted human to assume that his blind brother could ever lead so full a life as himself.

And what of the dog's hearing? Most people have at some time or other heard a dog howling with pleasure or sometimes with acute agony at some musical instrument or at a human voice. Amusing though this can be to the onlookers and embarrassing though it often is to the player of the musical instrument or the owner of the singing voice, there is a very special reason why the dog behaves in this way.

Careful observation will ascertain that he does not howl at every musical instrument or voice, not even at every musical instrument of a certain type or every voice of a certain range. The reason behind all this is that the dog does not hear as we hear, in exactly the same way as he does not see or scent as we do. His range is quite different and when he starts up this anguished howling it is because he has heard something we haven't. Something has either pleased him excessively or has grated on his ear to the degree that he has simply got to express his feelings vocally. Quite often it is a stringed instrument that has this effect on a dog, mainly because in the case of say a violin, the action of the bow being drawn across the strings creates a minute breeze which sets up extremely high pitched sounds far out of the range of human ears but easily accessible to dogs.

As the more scientifically minded of you will know, the atmosphere is full of sound waves, and the human range of contact with these is very limited indeed. The dog is differently placed, for he can hear a car engine above the noise of everyday living half a mile away, and cannot only distinguish the different notes of the different makes of cars, he can also, incredibly enough, distinguish different cars of the same make! This fascinating fact has been proved over and over again.

Talking of sounds in the atmosphere that the human ear cannot pick up brings us on to the subject of extra-sensory perception. Any observer of animals cannot readily disbelieve that this is indeed a fact. One has only to watch a dog or in fact any animal (particularly is this acute in a wild animal) where death has taken place, to know that this is true.

My Newfoundland bitch would never walk past a house where death had recently taken place. This caused quite a commotion the first time she dug her heels in over this and I had not realised the reason. However, one does not argue for very long with a 10-stoner, so, trusting to her wisdom that something was amiss, we turned round and went home. Soon after I learned that an old lady had passed away in the house that very morning. This happened once or twice again with the same dog on her walks, and when we had a bereavement in our own house, her cries of distress were so painful to us all that she was taken to kennels (the only time in her life) until after the funeral. Even then at her return she was obviously uneasy, and it was not until we had moved out of the house that she regained her usual aplomb.

Many people have experienced watching a dog 'seeing a ghost'. The hackles rise, the dog stares unwinkingly at a certain spot and often breaks out into shivering or hysterical barking. Rather spine-chilling if you happen to be alone in an isolated country house on a dark and windy night! It's easy enough to explain away this behaviour with 'mice under the floorboards' or 'creaking timbers', but those of you who have experienced this will agree that the dog has sensed a presence we would rather not know anything about, thank you very much!

Vibrations mean a great deal more to a dog than they do to us, and many dogs have a fear of walking over a space as in some Bath Halls where the space for the water is under the floorboards. Many dislike walking along a promenade or walking down open steps although they will go quite readily down filled in stairs. It is amazing that a dog should know when a well or cellar exists under a house when even the owners have not known of it. Yes, there are so many extraordinary things a dog knows by instinct or a sixth sense that we cannot keep pace with him.

All this indicates how a dog's view of life is influenced by many things that do not usually cross our own horizons. It is as well to remember when undertaking the care and welfare of a dog that his view is so different at times, and try to put ourselves up or down to his level whichever way one likes to look at it.

A dog's sense of taste is little use to him, judging by the way most of them swallow their food! Here again, most of the pleasure in food for the dog goes in the anticipatory savoury scents he receives from it, and the well-being he feels afterwards with a tummy comfortably satisfied. However, when working a dog in competitions, it is a good tip to bear in mind that the taste buds are closely connected with the scent organs, and a scent cloth taken in the mouth gives a double chance.

Touch, to a dog, appears to be slightly less important than it is to us. Even with a protecting beard and long, 'with-it' hair, it is doubtful whether we could tolerate a dog collar for long, yet the dog accepts it as part of life, putting up with some very rough treatment at times with stoic acceptance. Many unfortunate dogs have to put up with beatings of ferocity such as would kill a child of similar size. They survive to take another a week or so later and it does appear that physically the dog has a greater tolerance of hardship than man. The effect on the dog's mind of this type of treatment, however, is disastrous, and many a dog whose only crime has been a desire to do the job it was bred for – work – is rewarded by man in this way.

2 Looking After Your Dog

Basic Health: Exercise, Feeding, Grooming, Kennel Care:
Children and Dogs

Complementing the mental welfare of your dog is the physical side. This must necessarily be an important part of a dog's life, and particularly is this true of a dog you wish to train. A sound constitution, a healthy body, as well as an active mind, are the raw materials for our training plans, and it is as well to give careful thought to this side of things. It may seem like stating the obvious to say that you will have to look after your dog if you expect him to work well. Unhappily the obvious has to be rammed home at times, and a dog that is not fit should not be worked.

Dogs, even more than human beings, are influenced and governed by the early months of their lives. Whereas many a deprived child has survived an unhappy early life, even in many cases rising above adversity and environmental disaster to take a prominent and valued place in the world, the dog seems to lack initiative and constitution in later years if denied the opportunities for growth and development in his early months. It is what you put into the dog in food values during the first few months that will decide whether he will be constitutionally sound or not for the rest of his life. Perhaps it is because his rate of growth is so very rapid that once he drops behind he never seems to be able to catch up with himself later on.

The dog in the wild state caught his food and ate the entire animal. The construction of a dog's inside proves that he is a meat eater, able to take highly concentrated proteins and not needing anything like the quantity of fats and carbohydrates we feed on ourselves. Unlike ruminants like cattle and sheep, the dog's intestines are not geared to cope with continual feeding of vegetation such as grass. He gets his vegetable minerals and vitamins second-hand in the undigested part of the stomach contents of his kill. A certain amount of roots are eaten, and in this way the wild dog keeps himself alive and active.

Our own domesticated dogs, however, are not allowed to catch their own dinners, and have to rely on what we feed them. Unfortunately there is considerable ignorance in nutritional matters in human requirements, let alone in animal nutrition, and modern man consumes vast quantities of refined, devitalised matter largely because it is convenient. As a result we put up with increasingly tasteless food that has more and more synthetic flavouring in it to make it palatable, and the doctors' surgeries get more and more overflowing with patients who feel continually below par and even worse. Small wonder, when we take so little interest in what we are eating ourselves, that we fail to appreciate the very special needs of our pets!

To their credit, many owners are vaguely uneasy about the food their dogs are given, and try to balance their diets with supplements to make up for the goodness that should be present naturally. Providing supplements can, however, have a backlash, if there is evidence of imbalance. A far safer method is to feed good wholesome food, with as much of its natural vitamins and minerals in it as you can, i.e. raw red meat, offal (cooked if you prefer), wholemeal bread baked hard in the oven, or alternatively the best wholemeal biscuits you can afford.

Try to keep your supplements to natural products, i.e. bonemeal, fish liver and olive oils, wheat germ, yeast, seaweed, and a sprinkling of chopped parsley or other finely shredded green vegetable, and you won't go far wrong. As far as I know, the only item in this list that will upset metabolism if taken in excess is fish liver oil. However, a convenient and reasonably cheap way of buying this is in capsule form, and from weaning a puppy can safely take one daily.

Alter your new puppy's diet gradually if he has not been on one that agrees with your own ideas. Enquire of the breeder what he has been having and stay with that for a day or so, gradually introducing your own ideas until the change is complete. You will probably be feeding four times a day, which should be decreased gradually until at about 10–12 months old he is having just one meal, although some extremely large or small breeds thrive better on two smaller meals.

It is quite a good idea to fast the dog one day a week in the mildest weather, especially if you are rather too generous with your rations. Dogs that do a lot of travelling should be given a light meal after they have worked at the show. I take along half a pint of milk, a raw egg and a small cupful of biscuits for each dog before setting out on the long journey home. This light but sustaining meal suffices, and they settle down to sleep in the car.

Dogs should not be given snacks, as these cause havoc with their digestion. Table scraps are usually very good so long as they are additions to the dog's rations and not his main diet. Take out any white flour products, however, as these are even worse for your dog than they are for you. Never feed game or poultry bones, or cooked bones of any type. A marrow bone sawn by the butcher so the marrow is exposed is a great treat.

My own dogs are fed on raw butcher's meat four days a week, cooked tripe one day, and sometimes they have a delicious 'stew' made up of all the vegetable and fruit scraps, outer leaves, carrot ends, onion and apple peelings, etc., stewed into a thick soup. This is then poured over a mixture of meal and maize and is quite the most appreciated meal they have! On the day the meat ration looks a bit thin, their dinners are supplemented or fish or one of those 4 in. × 4 in. dog cakes of really hard wholemeal that can be purchased in the better type of corn chandlers.

Apart from their stew day, the food is fed dry, and even the stew is crumbly rather than wet. A great deal of damage is done to a dog's teeth and digestion by sloppy food.

There are some excellent tinned and complete meal products on the market for the occasional meal, but as they do not seem to give an adult dog's stomach or teeth anything to do they are best kept for standby feeding rather than the usual diet. If you live near a slaughter-house you can get paunches and heads, but these must be cleaned and cooked thoroughly – not a job everyone relishes. However, most butchers will help out if you approach them in a reasonable way, and you should have little difficulty in feeding one or two dogs with meat several days a week.

So much for the inner dog, as one might say. What about his spiritual comfort? All babies thrive on love, and the baby puppy that has had a lot of cuddling and demonstrative affection has a big advantage over a deprived one. That is why it is so very important that the lady of the house really enters into the spirit of the thing once it is decided that the breadwinner wants a dog. Whereas an adult dog grows dispirited and sometimes aggressive through lack of affection, a puppy will wilt. A woman is so much better than a man with small baby creatures, and she can give invaluable service in these early days. Her attitude towards a puppy will stay with it for the rest of its days. A happy, secure atmosphere creates confidence. The knowledge that it can run up to the lady of the house and lavish her with warm, milky kisses means a lot to a puppy. A harsh rebuff and his little world collapses. We have all seen and deplored the misery of little children denied their birthright of love and security, and the deprived puppy never seems to develop in the same way as his more fortunate brethren.

It is important to establish a pattern of behaviour early on that will act as a background of security to him, and here it is usually the woman who stays behind all day who can do the most to help. Routine is very important to a dog. Decide what is the most convenient time of the day to do certain tasks for him and try to keep to them. If his meal is in the evening he will start looking forward to it in the late afternoon. If you always take him out for walks at 7, 12 and 7, at 6.45, 11.45 and 6.45 he will stir from his sleep and wait at the door. This, to a dog, is security. He knows just what is happening and he knows where he is. It will help you later in your training when you must *be consistent* (Golden Rule No. 3) if you have acquired the habit earlier on. He must know what is expected of him, and he cannot if you alter your mind. He is not a thought reader.

One of the things that will create a sense of security in the dog is if he fits in well with the rest of the household. Children, in particular, are sometimes regarded as a very good reason why a dog should not be admitted to the house. On the other extreme, we have unfortunate puppies purchased as living toys for children who have no idea of how to look after them or treat them. These unfortunate animals frequently find themselves kicked outside once their baby fluffiness has disappeared. Left to fend for themselves, they become wanderers, often roaming for miles in search of food and companionship, frequently ending up under the wheels of a car and sometimes causing human injury or even death. The R.S.P.C.A and other animal welfare groups are rightly concerned with the large number of dogs that start off as playthings for children, and it is a national shame that there are so many irresponsible people around who take so casual a view of the duties of dog ownership.

It is a pity that children and dogs do not always mix well. Fundamentally, and without adult influence, the average child and the average puppy would adore to play together. However, both being excitable and tending to play rough, unsupervised companionship can quickly lead to trouble. Because they move about so quickly, jumping and racing around, children over-excite puppies, who soon use their needle-like teeth and claws in an effort to try and catch up with and hold on to their exciting new playmates.

Some children can be extremely unkind to puppies, even to the point of injuring them, and so obviously supervision is a 'must' to establish harmony. Because a child is a miniature human being, he must assume seniority in the playmate partnership. With that seniority, it must be carefully explained, comes responsibility. He is responsible for the behaviour of both himself and the puppy. It must be explained in a way a child can understand that the puppy 'doesn't know any better' than to get more and more excited, so he must take control himself and prevent this happening. Most children are delighted to be treated in this grown-up way of sharing the baby training of the puppy, particularly if they are allowed to give him his meals after an adult has prepared them, put the puppy to bed when it is time for him to have his rest, and go for adventurous walks and explorations in the garden. In this way they are doing things together and the child is learning to appreciate the companionship of a dog, a lesson he will value all his life. It is simply not fair to either if you leave a small child and a puppy together unsupervised.

It is important to realise that, when grown, a dog can be a source of danger to a child. No dog should be left with a baby, for instance. Many breeds of dog (Alsatians are notorious for this) are extremely playful and also extremely nosy, and while not meaning the slightest harm, it is a sad fact that many a dog has nudged a baby to see if it will get up and play. It nudges too hard on one occasion, with the tragic result that the baby is turned out of its pram and perhaps falls to its death. Uncontrollable jealousy for a new baby whose arrival has deprived him of his beloved owner's attention can also lead to tragedy, as we are so well aware. What is not so readily appreciated is the reason a devoted dog will sometimes turn and savage a child while playing. It is a fact of life that children under five years of age are extremely unsteady on their feet and frequently take a

A striking example
of mutual trust
between child and
dog: the author's
daughter Siobhan,
aged four, with
Seaanca Danny Boy

tumble, screaming as they fall. A dog uses the crouching position to attack, and in the excitement of a mad game can easily mistake the intentions behind a fall and a cry and will get his bite in first.

While not wishing to frighten the child away from dogs, it is as well to show him a dog's teeth and tell him that if he annoys the dog it will bite. He should be told that under no circumstances must he touch strange dogs and that if he sees a dog tied up he is to avoid it. Many a docile dog will turn into a ball of fury if tied to a fence and will attack all and sundry as they pass by. It goes without saying that time should be spent explaining to the child that a puppy is not a toy but a living creature of flesh and blood, nerve and sinew, with feelings as deep as his own, with his own rights and privileges. If possible, keep the dog's bed in a place inaccessible to the child or at least where you can keep an eye on what is happening. A dog suddenly woken from sleep is liable to attack.

Although you will be fighting a losing battle, constantly remind a child to keep his face away from dogs. Apart from any major danger of attack, a dog sniffs and chews all sorts of undesirable objects and could possibly convey bacteria through the mouth.

With reasonable care and training, child and dog can become devoted pals, but don't leave it to chance.

It is vitally important that at times the puppy and later the adult dog can get away from you. Make sure he has a comfortable bed, preferably right away from the hustle and bustle of a busy house – in a spare room or in his own kennel. A dog needs a great deal more sleep than we do, and to deny him this will make him bad tempered and too weary to take in training when we want him to concentrate. A kennel, if used, should be draught and damp proof, easily cleaned and ideally should have a double floor and lined walls. A tea chest or small raised bench should be included, with clean, comfortable bedding. Straw and hay are not very suitable for dogs as they encourage fleas. Newspaper is much better, or a small mat or blanket is much appreciated.

Grooming is important. If done daily, it gives you a chance of closely examining the dog to see if his condition is as good as it should be. A quick glance in the ears and eyes, at the nose, at the feet, and under the tail will tell you whether the dog is as well as he was yesterday. The best grooming instrument you will ever have is your hand, and a daily massage will stimulate his skin and loosen any dead fur. A good brisk brush with natural bristle against the growth of the fur will free the scurf and dead hair, and then a quick brush and comb the right way will smooth his wayward locks, and hey presto, he looks as smart as any. Obviously different coats need different specialist treatment, and your breed society will help you there.

Exercise is vital, particularly to the working dog. There should be no organised exercise for puppies until about eight months, when you can start your road work. Free running, however, is excellent and one should aim at a good half hour morning and evening.

Fresh air is essential and the healthiest dogs have had the air running through their coats all day and sometimes all night. A chain link outside run will see to this for you, but beware of the dog who gets over-excited and spends his day jumping up at the wire.

Of course you will want to find a good vet to whom you can take your problems and on whom you can rely in an emergency. It pays to shop around a little for one, for they vary in their knowledge and their interest. A vet who will not turn out in the middle of the night if you are in terrible trouble is not much use. But do your part, too, and don't call him up at Sunday lunch time for worm powders, please! Always keep to surgery hours except in dire circumstances. Have your puppies inoculated at 10–12 weeks against the canine killer diseases, have their boosters done regularly, and be advised on all matters of health by the expert. You pay for his knowledge and experience and it pays you to take note of what he says.

If you are unfortunate enough to have purchased a dog you suspect of having an hereditary defect, such as lameness, blindness, or epilepsy, consult your vet immediately. Unless the dog is in obvious pain, it should not be necessary for him to advise you to have him destroyed and with careful treatment the condition may be arrested (but not with blindness). Many are afflicted in some degree or other but they manage to live quite useful and happy lives. You must be guided by expert advice as to whether he should be trained and to what extent. Play fair with other dogs and dog owners, however, and do not breed from any animal known to be suffering from an hereditary disease.

What, then, are the minimum basic requirements for a dog's physical well being? I should not have thought it too difficult for dog owners to appreciate that every dog is surely entitled to decent sleeping accommodation, a constant supply of fresh, clean water, adequate exercise in the fresh air, and a good meal each day. It does not seem a great deal to ask for, but alas many a dog is denied even this minimum of attention. Why owners will not allow their dogs access to fresh drinking water is something that completely baffles me. Here is something that requires the minimum of attention and cost and yet, no, they actually ration the amount the dog is allowed to drink and he only has access to it at certain times during the day. Experiments have proved beyond any doubt that (1) a dog drinks far more if water is rationed in this way, and (2) brain damage is the ultimate result of denying the dog access to water over a period of time. So do see that your dog can always get to his water bowl and that it is always filled.

As far as sleeping accommodation goes, much depends on whether the dog sleeps indoors or out. The indoor dog will appreciate a bed of his own and this is useful for training purposes. When you want him from under your feet you can always suggest bed. However, a bed is not essential as most modern houses are reasonably draught-proof and, given his freedom, the dog will pick the most comfortable place in it for his own. It is far more likely that the indoor dog will suffer from the heating of the house and possibly lack of ventilation. Dogs require more air than we do, and if left in the kitchen, which many dogs are, a window should be left open and where possible the heating turned off. It is most improbable that a dog sleeping indoors will suffer from cold, but highly likely he will be doped with fumes from heating.

Outdoor kennels should be periodically examined to ensure that they are damp- and draught-proof. A healthy dog can put up with intense cold, but dampness and draughts will break down the constitution of a sound dog quicker than anything. Fresh air is a basic requirement of any dog, and the dog that lives most of his life outside has a bloom that is denied the over-cosseted family pet. All dogs require exercise in the fresh air; never mind a drop of rain, that won't hurt him and he should be taken out as often as practical.

Feet are an extremely important part of a working dog, and it is quite horrifying to see the dreadful splayed feet, weak pasterns and spindley legs of some so-called 'beauty' dogs in the Working Dog group at the shows. Controlled road work is needed for strong feet and legs, and from nine months onwards this is an essential daily chore. Puppies should never be given road work, but allowed to exercise themselves in a safe place to their heart's content. A free country run is also a daily necessity for every adult dog, and if you can arrange for an occasional swim he will be in clover.

Like an army, a dog marches through life on its stomach and its feet, and if these are neglected the battles of life are hard indeed to fight.

Although I don't want to dwell for long on this side of things, it is worth while studying the make-up of the dog. With its small stomach and fang-like teeth it is obviously constructed to eat meat and to tear its food into lumps small enough to swallow without much chewing. The extremely strong chemicals in the digestive system break down these lumps and utilise the goodness from them. Unlike cattle, the dog does not need to eat all day, and is better served if given one small meal of high protein food per day. His meals should consist of at least 75 per cent fresh raw meat. The mixing of meat and biscuit (a widely held practice) is not good for the dog's digestion and a much more satisfactory way of feeding is to give meat four or five times a week and meatless meals the other days.

There comes a time, dreaded by all who love their dogs, when we must part from our friends. To some, death comes after a life-time enjoyed to the full, and time alone denies us any further years. Perhaps we find the dog, as I found one old friend of mine, asleep, as I thought, one morning in his usual resting place. It was only when I examined him further that I realised he would never stir again. If the end comes as peacefully as this, after many devoted years, the latter few of which we have noticed the old dog growing slower in his steps, more reluctant to go for walks these days, dimmer in the eye, we should be thankful for them that the passing was so sweet. Death comes as the end to all living creatures. None can escape but if we could only guarantee our own end and those of our dear ones as peaceful as this, devoid of suffering or fear, dropping into sleep and from sleep to death, we would be content in our minds.

Too many people as well as animals meet violent, horrible deaths, some lingering in suffering until only death releases them. It is up to all animal lovers to see that every precaution is taken to avoid accidents or diseases which lead to death. Occasionally a dog we had thought was healthy dies young. I always feel so sorry for the owners when this happens, for the shock and bewilderment takes a time to get over.

In the case of a dog that is growing obviously very old, unless veterinary advice is to the contrary, I see no justification for destruction simply because the signs of age are becoming more acute. Signs such as dimmed vision, teeth falling out, deafness, slowness of movement, etc., will not distress the dog whose whole structure now is adapted to the slowing down of pace. If, however, there is incurable internal trouble or the dog is obviously distressed with extreme age, for which there is, alas, no cure, one must think carefully what is best for the dog – whether oblivion would be merciful, or whether there is still any joy for him in life.

If one has to decide, and the decision, alas, has to come from the one who loves him best, that oblivion would now be the kindest, my advice is to call your veterinary surgeon and discuss the matter with him. If he agrees, by far the kindest way of destruction is to have the vet visit you at your home, have the dog quietly at your side and let the vet inject into the dog's front leg while you are with him. If the dog is very old or very ill, he will be dead before the needle is withdrawn. Try to show no distress until life is extinct. It is extremely unkind to distress an animal during this last act and by your calm behaviour he will not be aware of anything unusual. Only by showing emotion and distress can you harm him at this stage.

The vet will listen to his heart to confirm that death has taken place. He will probably suggest he takes the body. By all means agree, and even if he does not suggest it, ask him if he will do this additional service for you. If you prefer, you can, of course, bury the body in your garden, but personally I am not very keen on the idea, particularly if you have children or other animals or are likely to have another dog, which I sincerely hope you will.

Some people go to very elaborate funeral arrangements and erect monumental stones in memory of their pets. A far greater memorial in my opinion is to spend time, care, love and money on some other animal's welfare and thus repay to the animal kingdom some of the debt you owe for so much devotion from one of its members.

We cannot help showing our grief at the death of our friends, and the time for this is immediately after their death. Consolation lies in the fact that his life in your hands was a happy, full one. You did everything in his lifetime to return his love and trust. In the nature of things, dogs must always be expected to die before their owners. It is a sad dog indeed who outlives his beloved master, and we should not wish him to change places with us in this matter. To be able to look back on so many happy memories of companionship and devotion we are indeed fortunate. When one considers the misery in the lives of many, many poor children and even more pitiful animals we should be thankful that our own beloved pet had a good life with us.

When the rawness of parting has dimmed and the emptiness of the house strikes more and more, think seriously about having another dog. Take your time, don't jump into anything that may be regretted later on. Don't expect your next dog to be anything like the one you have just lost. He won't be, but, given the opportunity, he will develop his own character and charm, and will try his best to ease the ache that will always be there, just a little, for every dog you ever lose, however long ago it happened. Sometimes we hear people say, 'I'll never have another dog. I could never go through all that unhappiness of losing another one.' How foolish to remember only the unhappiness of parting when there are so many years of happy memories to help ease the pain. These people deny themselves the happiness and consolation that a new wet nose and a new warm tongue can bring.

3 Choosing Your Puppy

Early Days: General Basic Work: Socialising and Safety

When we consider that a dog will probably be part of our lives for ten to fifteen years, dependent upon us for bed, board, exercise and happiness, it is well worth while spending considerable time and thought on exactly what type of dog we should choose.

Sometimes, of course, kind-hearted persons have dogs wished on them. Perhaps they rescue a dog from unhappy circumstances, or give a good home to an unfortunate animal (of whom, alas, there are so many!) who has been turned out when the first attractive weeks of puppyhood have worn off or the time for licensing has come round. To these warm-hearted folk I can only say I hope the dog repays you for all you have done for it. I am sure if the scars of any experience it has had previous to your ownership are not too deep it will repay you in devotion for all your trouble.

In most of these cases the dog settles well and all are pleased with the arrangement. There can be some circumstances, however, where there is trouble from the start. An adult dog may have acquired bad habits that are difficult to eradicate, or may be suffering from some physical weakness owing to its unfortunate start in life and premature death ensues. If one is prepared to take these risks, however, and consult a veterinary surgeon immediately on receipt of a dog from a 'home' or 'pound', there can surely be no greater satisfaction to the true dog lover than to give a loving home to an outcast that has never known individual care and attention. Any branch of the R.S.P.C.A., any local dogs' home or kennels, any police station, will be happy to furnish advice as to how and where such dogs are obtainable to genuine good homes.

However, if your decision, as is that of most people, is to have a puppy and bring it up to your own ways from the start, and to enjoy its development through the various stages of its life, some consideration must be given to what can be expected when the salad days of puppyhood have gone.

Firstly, having assured ourselves that we can give a dog a good home, we must ask ourselves (1) What facilities we have for keeping a dog? (2) What do we want a dog for? (3) Do we want a mongrel or pedigree, dog or bitch?

Obviously there are certain elementary essentials that all dogs require. The first and most important one, in my opinion, is that the dog is anticipated with pleasure by the person who will have it for the bulk of its lifetime. I do not necessarily mean its owner, who may have to go out to work all day and leave it in someone else's charge (in almost every case, the wife of the owner). Unless this person is not only prepared but cheerfully willing to undertake the welfare of the dog during its owner's absence, I personally feel that it is extremely unfair to introduce a dog into an atmosphere where its very presence may be a constant irritation.

This may seem an obvious point to make, but I am afraid it is all too often made light of in the excitement of purchasing a dog, and is the forerunner of constant trouble.

Mongrel or pedigree? It does not make a ha'porth of difference with regard to intelligence or health, which will be exactly what breeding, rearing and environment allow, but it is as well to know what lies behind your dog as regard to size and temperament. It can be very disconcerting when that dear little pup, mothered by a bitch of terrier proportions and sweet disposition, grows up to be a hulking great monster with a positively anti-social streak! With a pedigree animal you can at least be sure of the size it should reach if nothing else. Many people take pride in the animal's background, and it is a sad fact that a well-bred dog, purchased at a fair price, usually stands more chance of being well cared for than one whose ancestry is discreetly veiled and is given away for next to nothing. Although again, I have known scores of mongrels who lived like kings and had a far happier and fuller life than their well-bred show brethren who lived a discontented kennel life, high-lighted only by days of uncomfortable journeys to and from a show bench.

Now, as to why you want a dog. Is the dog to be a treasured family pet, a constant companion of children? Is it to be owned by an energetic sort of person who loves long country walks and is prepared to spend several hours a week with his canine pal? Is it to be used for some purpose such as breed showing, competitive Obedience or Working Trials? Is it to be the loved companion of some elderly lady living in a town flat, or the dog to 'look after' a country estate and go with his master on occasional shoots and then wait patiently for him in the local pub during a darts match? How much time can we spend grooming our dog?

It is worth while asking ourselves exactly why we want the dog, what sort of person we are, and what sort of dog would suit us best. In this way we should be able to arrive at some indication as to what breed would suit our purpose best. Remember that all dogs originally were bred for a purpose, and it is up to us as prospective owners to find the type of dog bred as near as we can for the purpose we want. After all, we would not buy a Shetland pony if we had hopes of winning the Grand National. Neither would we buy a hotted up two-seater to take the family touring. The purchase of a dog should be given adequate consideration and then we can hope for many happy years with, and for, the dog of our choice.

To give some sort of guide, I am listing some of the more usual breeds, their purpose in life, and my opinion of them.

When choosing a puppy, consider how much it will grow. Bessie, the mongrel, and Mandy, a Newfoundland pup, seem well matched for happy play together. But the picture at the bottom was taken only one year later

WORKING GROUP
Bred to work. Dogs for people prepared to spend considerable time in training and exercise. They include:

Alsatians (German Shepherd Dogs): the most popular breed registered with the Kennel Club. Unfortunately for the breed its popularity has made it the victim of people who think it clever to own a big dog even though they have no intention of doing anything with it once they have purchased it. One cannot expect any dog, least of all a dog with the alert intelligence and desire to work that this breed possesses, to go into a coma throughout most of its life and only 'come to' on the few occasions when required to be shown off to impress friends. It is an extraordinary thing that many 'crimes' in the canine calendar are attributed to this breed which in fact they have not committed, while most deeds of heroism are credited in certain areas of the popular press to mongrels – a delegation of vice and virtue which rather pleases me for the mongrels' sake, but which is greeted with justifiable protest from Alsatian lovers.

Collies (Rough, Smooth and Shetland Sheepdogs): charming dogs which can make delightful companions without needing too much to occupy their minds.

Bearded Collies: dogs of immense charm and character. Prefer an outlet for their wide-awake brains. Need especially careful grooming.

Old English Sheepdogs: also must be groomed with great care. Not over-endowed with much in the way of 'little grey cells'.

Border Collies (Sheepdogs): long regarded by the shepherd as the most sagacious of them all. Will usually adapt well to a pet home, although they are at their happiest when given a job of work to do. In some cases can turn extremely awkward if their lively minds and spritely bodies are not given adequate exercise. My own great favourites and, in my opinion, second to none in their devotion and intelligence.

Great Danes, Bullmastiffs, Dobermanns, Rottweilers: not for the average pet home, but grand if you are a rough, tough type with plenty of space and time to exercise their minds and bodies.

Samoyeds: noisy; glamour boys.

Boxers: these boisterous dogs never know when to grow up.

Corgis: gay but stubborn.

Groenendaels: promising.

Briards: very promising, and great characters.

UTILITY GROUP
Almost all from this group make ideal family pets and breed show dogs. Included are:

Poodles (Miniature and Toys): noisy and highly strung. (Standard): sensible and trainable.

Bulldogs, Chows.

Dalmatians: need a lot of exercise.
Boston Terriers, French Bulldogs, Keeshonds: intelligent but independent.
Schipperkes, Schnauzers: trainable.
Lhasa Apsos, Shih Tzus, and Tibetan Spaniels: delightful.

GUNDOGS
Ideal companions. Usually extremely reliable with children, although lack of exercise and control can make them excessively boisterous. The group includes:
Retrievers (Golden, Labrador, Flat Coated, Curly Coated).
Spaniels (Cocker, Springer, Clumber, American, Sussex, Irish Water, Field).
Pointers and German Short Haired Pointers, Setters (Gordon, English, Irish).

TERRIERS
Once a terrier man, always a terrier man. There is something about these gay little horrors with their wicked gleaming eyes that tweaks the heart, and many a brawny giant has dropped the unashamed tear at the passing of his terrier. Plucky to the extreme, they are game for anything. In my own personal experience have been wonderful with children, but the confirmed enemies of postmen, cats and many other innocent crossers of their path! Included are:
Airedales, Bull, Bedlington, Border, Australian, Dandie Dinmont, Jack Russell (not recognised by the Kennel Club), *Irish, Welsh, Staffordshire Bull, Fox, Cairn, West Highland White, Norfolk, Norwich, Manchester, Sealyham, Skye, Kerry Blue, Lakeland, Soft Coated Wheaten.*

TOY DOGS
Ideal for people of restricted movement and space. Given the opportunity, though, are game for anything, and it is a lovely sight to see a pack of Papillons or Chihuahuas chasing over the fields in great glee and at surprising speed. However, although they are bright little things they are not easy to train for competitive work unless you happen to be a contortionist. Think of all that back bending! They include:
Pekingese, Miniature Pinscher, Italian Greyhound, King Charles Spaniel, Papillon, Pomeranian, Chihuahua, Cavalier, Dachshund, Pug, Griffon, Maltese, English Toy Terrier, Japanese, Yorkshire Terrier.

BIG BREEDS
Dogs for people with plenty of money to feed them! It is grossly unfair to try to keep this type of dog on short rations, particularly in the formative months. If you are prepared to spend money you will probably have a glorious pet, a show piece to turn your humble house into a stately home.

But beware of occasional bad temperaments with large dogs – you could get eaten! Breeds included are:
Newfoundland, St. Bernard, Mastiff, Pyrenean.

HOUNDS

Need a great deal of physical exercise to keep them in trim. They are spectacular looking dogs, but, apart from the smaller varieties such as Beagles, are not ideally suited to home life. They include the following:
Irish Wolf, Deerhound, Basset, Rhodesian Ridgeback, Saluki, Borzoi, Greyhound, Whippet, Beagle, Elkhound, Bloodhound, Finnish Spitz, Basenji, Afghan, Fox, Harrier (not recognised by the Kennel Club).

Having made your choice of the type of dog you want, the next step is to contact a reputable breeder of the type chosen. A glance through the advertisements in the canine press (*Dog World* and *Our Dogs*), or the better type of country magazine (*The Field, Country Life*, etc.) will give you some idea of the price these dogs can fetch. There will be a considerable price range of pedigree dogs in each breed because naturally one must expect to pay more for a puppy from a line which has achieved success in the show or Obedience ring or at Field or Working Trials, and which is a possibility for top honours itself.

If you do not want to 'beauty' show the dog you should make this quite clear to the breeder of your choice, who will then probably pick you out a well-bred puppy carrying some fault which debars him from being a top-flight show dog, but which nevertheless carries all the characteristics of the breed that you have so admired.

If possible have a good look at both the sire and the dam of the puppies offered for sale. From them you will gain some reasonable idea of the eventual colouring, type and temperament that you can expect from the puppies. Remember that some breeds change colour from puppyhood onwards, ears become erect at a later date and tails drop. If there is an outstanding weakness in either parents this will be passed on to some of the puppies, and may well be carried by them to the next generation.

If the adult dogs are in good condition and clean, it is reasonable to assume that the puppies are likewise and in good health. Examine them quietly from a distance. Do not interfere with their play, but watch carefully to see how they react. Are they sound asleep snoring contentedly? Do they come tumbling out of the nest to see what is going on? Are their little bodies well rounded, with sturdy limbs and gaily held tails? Look out for obvious faults such as turned-in feet in breeds that are not supposed to have them, poor shoulder placement, etc., and beware of any puppies with running noses and eyes (unless of course you want to rescue them). They may well be heading for distemper.

A puppy with a very large tummy has been poorly weaned. Excessive pinching of the back quarters can indicate worms or worse. Carefully and quickly examine the puppy's mouth for obvious faults such as an over-shot or under-shot jaw. Feel the base of the spine in breeds that are supposed to have low-lying tails and see whether the tail is low set. Most puppies carry their tails gaily, and it is no indication at this stage how the tail will eventually hang. Examine the coat for signs of harshness and the skin for any rashes or blemishes which may indicate mange or other skin disorders. See the eyes are clear and bright and the nose and mouth attractively moist. Finally put the puppy of your choice down, offer him a crumpled up piece of paper or a little stick and see if he shows any interest in having a game with you. If he obviously wants to and likes you, he is the pup for you!

A word about whether to choose a dog or a bitch. One the whole I think a bitch is slightly more home-loving than a dog, but be prepared for her to come into season twice a year, when precautions must be taken to keep her away from possible suitors. Dog or bitch, though, it will make little difference to the trust and devotion you can expect in return for your care and love.

Once you have purchased your puppy you cannot start too soon on what I term 'socialising' him. This is not training but is merely getting him used to your way of life, guiding him gently so that he fits in comfortably with the household without being allowed to disrupt things. Remember he knows nothing at this point about you, your home and garden, or about the world in general, and you must help him to understand.

The beauty of puppy socialising is that you do not have to do anything except carry on with your life and allow the puppy to fit in with you. There is no question of 'training', 'correction', or any of these other sterner-sounding aspects of life. You merely help him, remembering, always Golden Rule No 1: *Prevention is Better than Cure*. From the start, prevent him from making himself a nuisance to you, and it will never occur to him to do so. Get him into his routine straight away. Select times for meals, for rests, for play periods, and stick to them. For the first day or so, just let him get used to you and the others in the household, let him into the rooms he will be permitted to use, and the garden, introduce him to other pets you have, and show him how delightful you think he is in every way possible. If you have an older dog, confine your ecstasies over the new puppy to when the other dog is out of earshot, and make a special fuss of the older dog whenever the two are together. The last thing you want is the older dog's nose pushed out of joint.

Start socialising the puppy for car travelling. On the way home, the new owner should hold the puppy on his knee wrapped in a suitable rug and should arm himself with a roll of kitchen paper towelling in case of accidents. If you prefer, put the puppy in a box at your feet and talk to him to reassure him, but don't let the puppy look out of the window, for the moving scenery will frighten him. Ask the driver to take it easy on corners, with no quick jerky movements starting and stopping.

Later on the dog will have to learn to lie down quietly in the car whilst you are driving. Start early on by putting the puppy in a stationary car on several occasions. When he settles well, drive a few yards. Then build up to very short journeys. Introduce him gradually to car travel and he will soon begin to enjoy it. Fear makes dogs sick quicker than anything, so try to help him overcome his natural apprehension until he regards a ride in the car as a treat. Adult dogs that are poor travellers should be confined to a wired-in section of the car, liberally lined with plastic sheeting and newspaper, and should not be fed for twelve hours before a journey. However, if the approach is sensible with a young puppy, the adult dog seldom suffers from car sickness.

If your dog jumps out of a car before it is told to, you should teach it the meaning of the command 'Stay'. Then, when you say this, it will not matter whether the dog is at home, in the fields or in your car, he will obey the command he knows and understands. Another method of ensuring that the dog stays in the car until you are ready for him to leave is to tie him up. Have a special fitment put in the car and tie him short on a leather lead with a leather collar. Do not tie the lead to a door as the dog could possibly be injured and never under any circumstances leave a dog in a car or anywhere else in a chain collar.

Back to our newly-arrived puppy. Start house training immediately. He will need to be carried outside after every meal and drink, whenever he wakes up, and whenever he has a particularly earnest expression on his face. You will soon learn to read the signs. Of course at first he will have no idea why he is being taken outside apart from the chance to play and explore. But by patience and explanation to him that he is out there to 'Spend a Penny' or some similar command, he will come to understand that something is expected of him, although he has little idea what. Time after time you will stand outside with him without results, only to bring him in for him to bob down and make a pool. Pick him up as quickly as you can without frightening him and rush him outside, giving your command. If you manage to get a trickle outside give lavish praise. The time will come when quite by accident he does perform outside. When he does, croon your command to him in delighted tones and give extra special praise. Confine the puppy to an area of easily washed floor when you can't be with him.

Remember a puppy's inside is so very immature he simply can't wait, so you will have to jump to it if you want to save yourself a mess. Never, ever, rub a puppy's nose in its mess. This is both cruel and revolting, and serves no useful purpose. Just blame yourself for being too slow on the uptake.

Puppies in strange surroundings frequently howl at night. You would not, at least I hope you would not, beat a human baby for crying in the night, and I hope you will not be so unkind to your baby puppy. He has just left his mother and litter companions, and doesn't like being on his own. Find an old cuddly toy, or tie up an old woolly jumper to resemble a 'body' and give it to him to snuggle up to. A pleasantly warm (not hot) water bottle well wrapped up is a great comfort, and often a clock with a loud tick works magic. If he persists after you have made him as comfortable as possible you will have to stuff cotton wool in your ears and leave him to it. The chances are he will settle down quite soon once he realises that he is not going to get you back again. The more you go back to him the longer he will keep on.

If things don't improve at all after a few nights you can try hiding behind the door until he lets out his protest and then speaking very sharply to him, 'Be quiet', 'No', 'Bad dog', etc. and repeat as often as necessary. You may have to spend a sleepless night or two doing this, but far better a sleepless night now than a lifetime of having a dog that persists in barking every time you leave it.

One of the things that seems to worry some people a lot is a puppy that jumps up. A simple way of curing this is to ignore him when he does. Make a great fuss of him when he greets you so long as his four feet are on the ground. When he raises himself on two feet, stop the fuss. Immediately four feet go on the ground again renew it. It takes about two or three sessions of a few minutes each for an average intelligent puppy to get the message – and consequently saves a lifetime of nagging and annoyance on your part and bewilderment on the dog's part, because frankly the average dog usually has no idea at all what it has done wrong when the average dog owner corrects it!

When your puppy has had his inoculations you can start taking him out (at fourteen weeks). By now he should be fitting in well with the routine of the house. He should be reasonably reliable during the day, but still liable to wet the floor occasionally at night. He should have learned to greet visitors with restrained interest and you yourself with unrestrained enthusiasm. He should be capable of going short journeys in the car without being sick, and should know there are certain things he has to leave alone. Of course if you are foolish enough to risk your best nylons, that's your misfortune, but he should be learning now that he can chew up his own toys but not yours! Provide him with suitable material to cut his teeth on. They really hurt until about five months old, and he will have to use something. If you don't provide a large bone or a piece of really hard wood he will eat the lino or chew the chair legs.

Now is the time to get him used to a soft leather collar. Simply put the collar on without any fuss and then walk straight out into the garden for a game with him. The chances are he will not even notice he has it on. If he does scratch at it, distract his attention with some exciting new toy or give him his dinner, and he will soon grow accustomed to having it on. Leave it on for increasingly long periods during the day (never at night or when he is unsupervised). When he is quite used to it, attach a lead to it and see what happens. It may be that he takes no notice, but the chances are he will take quite a bit. He may sit down and look puzzled. He may go frantic.

Remember that up to now his entire 'training' has been done by tone of voice, a cross tone for 'correction', and lavish praise when he has done something clever. For the first time now he is up against physical restraint. If he merely sits down, slacken the lead by taking a pace up to him and call him in a very endearing tone. If he comes to be comforted, he is responding nicely. Back away a pace and call him again. Don't put any pressure on the lead at all. Keep calling him to you until he ignores the lead altogether. Then gradually encourage him to walk with you. If he makes a sudden lunge, slacken the lead so that the pressure is at a minimum. If necessary let him take you for a walk the first few times until he gets used to gentle pressure. Afterwards, you can persuade him to go where you want.

All this early work is done in the familiar background of your garden. Don't try this outside yet. When you want to take him out put his collar and lead on, pick him up and carry him wherever you are going. An ideal place to take him is to some quiet shops (not to do the shopping). Let him see traffic but don't plunge him straight into it. Let him see people and buildings, but all from the safety of your arms. Try his reaction to being put down in an unfamiliar place such as a park or other quiet spot. See how you get on with your lead training in the park. When he will walk quite happily on the lead here, then is the time to introduce him to traffic from a distance and gradually to the roads. However, at four months old he certainly won't be able to walk far, and you must still be prepared to carry him most of the way.

By this time he will, of course, have learnt the meaning of the words I mentioned in chapter 1 : his name, and most of the negative words. 'Come' is a very useful word and should be taught very early on. It is not a competition recall, it merely means 'Come as fast as you can because I want to give you a kiss and a cuddle'. Practise this on the lead now in the park. You can also teach him to sit by holding your right hand over his head and giving the command 'Sit'. Most puppies over-balance in their curiosity when your hand goes up and you have a lovely puppy 'Sit'. If he doesn't respond to this, gently press his bottom to the floor as you say the word.

A word now about safety. Never, at any stage in the dog's life and however highly trained you think he is, allow a situation whereby if the dog does happen to disobey you for any reason, or is given a fright, it is possible for him to get killed. It is not clever to walk a dog off the lead where there is danger from cars. In her heyday, one of my dogs has been the top winning Obedience bitch in the country, but I would no more dream of allowing her to walk off the lead along the road than I would dream of allowing my four-year-old daughter to take herself off to nursery school each day. There are some things that are just not worth the risk. A car backfiring, someone pushing past to catch a bus, a passing cat, a squealing of brakes and the accompanying startled reaction of nearby pedestrians, and your dog's attention is diverted. One mistake and he is under the wheels of the nearest car. Keep him on the lead always except when you know it is absolutely safe for him to be free.

4 It's a Mad, Mad World

Competitive Enthusiasts: The Right Attitude to Approaching
Competition

I want to pass on now to competitive work and the training involved. Every
weekend, hundreds of enthusiasts pack their picnic baskets, their children
and, most important of all, their dogs, and set out by car or rail with high
hopes and determination to pit their skill and training against all comers in
what is fast becoming one of the most absorbing and most popular of
present day sports – competitive dog obedience.

What is the attraction? Obviously the fact that this is a participant rather
than an armchair hobby has a lot to do with it. There are few more readily
available opportunities for the average man in the street to take part in an
exercise requiring physical and mental skill than competitive dog training.
As a nation of dog lovers, we do, of course, regard it as a bonus that our
beloved pets are the star attractions.

Competitive dog obedience is still one of the sports where one can
believe virtue and skill get their just rewards. It is not easy to cheat
undetected in the Obedience ring, and, to their credit, few try. A genuine
admiration for a good dog, well trained and presented, seems to pervade,
perhaps because we all know the difficulties in getting to the top. Thus, the
harder one tries, the more successful one can expect to become. Some
trainers have a large number of dogs all capable of doing well in their class,
with others it is a struggle to get anywhere with one, but at least one feels
one starts off with an equal chance, and with perseverance can triumph.

You don't have to be wealthy to take part, although obviously money
helps, especially if you intend travelling. However, people involved in
other sports would be astonished if they knew the lengths the real
Obedience enthusiast will go to in order to get to the shows. No sacrifice is
too great once the bug has bitten hard. It is no secret among certain die-
hards that the quality and style of the evening meal on the way home
depends on the results of the day! Success means egg and chips on the
motorway. No place, and it is a cheese roll!

To the outsider, the Obedience enthusiast must appear in need of having
his head examined. Who, in his right mind, would travel hundreds of miles
every week, missing one and sometimes two nights' sleep, to stand all day
in the pouring rain (it always seems to pour with rain at the outdoor shows,
which carry on regardless) for the privilege of five minutes in the ring with
a dog at one's heels? Yet hundreds do, and proof of the growing hold it has
are the ever-increasing entries and the subsequent problems they create.

L. A. Pearce,
Chairman of the
Kennel Club
Obedience Council,
presents the author
with an oil painting
at Crufts. The
painting, by Olive
Openshawe, was a
gift donated by
admirers of
Obedience
Champion Seaanca
Fern on her
retirement from the
Show Ring, aged 10

The financial rewards are very slight – indeed my Obedience Champion Seaanca Fern, top winner, certainly did not pay her way – but the rewards in thrills (sometimes sad spills) and sense of achievement are inestimable.

The initial outlay is negligible – in fact you probably have your raw material sunning himself in the garden just now or dozing contentedly in the best armchair, but the price increases as your enthusiasm grows. The beauty about competitive Obedience as opposed to any other form of dog sport in the United Kingdom is that literally any old dog will do. Even that decrepit old hearthrug of a mongrel who barely knows who his mother is and who looks slightly hurt if you happen to mention his dad, is fully

Obedience Champion Seaanca Fern: Olive Openshawe's oil portrait. Seaanca Fern was bred by Ron Brookes entitled to take his place in the august Kennel Club roll of 'others', namely the Obedience Register, as opposed to that reserved for the elite breed 'gentlemen'. Here there are scores of dogs entered with the words 'further details unknown' printed beside them. Some of these 'pedigree unknowns' have risen to the dizziest of heights, for brains and willingness are not the prerogative of blue blood. Indeed some winners of the Supreme Obedience Championship at Crufts cast a veil over their ancestors, so you can see there is no end to the possibilities of even the humblest of pets.

Obviously, however, one cuts one's suit according to one's cloth, and it would be foolish indeed to think silk purses could be made out of every sow's ear. The better the working background of your dog, the better advantage you are giving yourself. Many of today's top Alsatian and Border Collie Obedience Champions can trace their way back through an impressive line of equally famous ancestors, albeit they have won their honours in different fields, such as Police work, working trials or sheepdog trials.

The chief thing is, however, that alone of all dog sports competitive Obedience in this country is open to all dogs, big, small, pedigree, crossbred, young, old, entire or neutered, and therein lies its greatest attraction. Other countries, such as the U.S.A., Canada and the Republic of Ireland, which limit Obedience to certain breeds, are dismally behind us in their standards and visitors from these countries can hardly believe their eyes when they see our dogs in action. I was told recently by a foreign judge that some of our Class A dogs could probably beat every champion in his country!

Another important point to remember is that Obedience here is open to all handlers. You don't have to be a professional to win, in fact owner/handlers are almost invariably the rule, the occasional professional being the odd man out. You don't have to be an athlete or even particularly fit and agile to compete – in fact expectant mothers, both human and canine, have been especially successful at this game! In Working Trials, however, which make big demands on physique of handler and dog, you are at a great disadvantage with a physical handicap, and it is virtually impossible for certain breeds of dogs to win.

In competitive Obedience, however, many people enjoy themselves each week despite quite serious injuries and ill-health. I even saw a three-legged dog once compete in Obedience, and although I didn't much enjoy the spectacle, I must admit the dog appeared to cope with the minimum of effort.

No, you don't have to rush out and buy yourself a special dog for Obedience. With skilful training, any healthy, reasonably intelligent dog can gain places at Obedience competitions so long as the handler has sufficient enthusiasm and willingness to learn by his mistakes.

Equipment again is kept to the minimum. A carefully welded chain slip collar of the right size, a good quality leather lead with a bolt fastening (or its cheaper nylon equivalent), a wooden dumb-bell, a small article for scent, and you are away. Gumboots, mackintosh and waterproof headwear are, of course, essentials for the handler, as most of the shows are held in typical British summer weather amid the pouring rain.

Figure 1. Four different types of lead fastenings

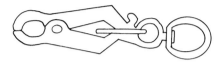

(*a*) The scissor fastening. The pressure from the dog comes on the weakest point of this clip, at the opening

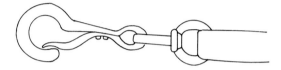

(*b*) The bill hook. Extra strong pressure from the dog could open this hook. Again, the pressure is on a vital part of the clip

(*c*) A variation of the bill hook but stronger with an inner spring. This type of hook together with (*b*) must never be left lying on the ground where the dog may step on it. It will dig deep into the pad and cause acute pain

(*d*) By far the most satisfactory type of fastening. The bolt fastening. Pressure is taken on the strongest part of the clip and there is nothing to damage the dog's foot if he steps on it

Training clubs and canine societies with training sections flourish throughout the country, and no one should have any difficulty in contacting one within reach. Many of the trainers at these clubs are enthusiastic rather than skilful, but by using his own initiative and common sense the new recruit can gain a lot of valuable dog information which will stand him in good stead. He will absorb atmosphere, which is very important, and so will his dog. They will both get used to the strange lingo of the dog ring, sounding as it does a cross between the parade ground ('Forward', 'Left About Turn', 'At the Double', etc.) and a Women's Institute talk by the vicar on family problems ('Now don't worry, my dear, just give him plenty of encouragement'). One wonders what he'll do then, he's bad enough now with discouragement!

Here at the club you will meet lots of people all talking dogs. Suggestions are put forward for each and every problem you are likely to come across and, if you are lucky, some of them will actually work. Like most other participant sports and hobbies, the attraction grows as one's knowledge increases, and the more eager one is to progress.

Obedience handlers are a strange breed. In time they don't even look like the rest of the population. The permanently stiff shoulders of one handler contrast curiously with the india-rubber-like qualities of the next, who bows to his dog at every end and turn in a frantic effort to keep his dog's disdainful attention. The revolving kneecaps and twitching fingers of others, the perpetual toothy grin which some dogs demand of their handlers, the hanging heads and the clicking heels, the ballet movements and the strange shoe-sticking-to-the-floor routines in some of the about turns at the double surely place Obedience dog handlers apart from the rest of the human race!

The almost universal uniform of the dog handler is slacks and sweater, the outline usually spoilt by curious bulges in the most astonishing places. No one worries over-much about this, as scent articles have to be put somewhere!

High among the hazards of competing in the Obedience ring is the possibility of getting bitten. Not by the dogs, I must hasten to say, for there are few if any really vicious dogs at the shows, and those that can give a painful nip are usually either in the handler's car when not actually in the ring or tied up well away from the main part of the show where they can only annoy anyone who deliberately annoys them first.

Far more likely is the possibility of getting your head bitten off by humans at dog shows, especially if you make some fatuous remark just as they are coming out of the ring after a disastrous round! To their credit, few handlers blame their dogs on these occasions, but they are often ready for trouble, so look out! At one Championship show I was severely bitten by an apparently ownerless small boy. The incident occurred when I tried to persuade him to descend a flight of perilous stone steps he had climbed.

After noisy protest he came down only to give my helping hand a severe bite as we reached the bottom.

People take up Obedience dog training for a variety of reasons. Many have an uncontrollable dog which they take in desperation to the local dog training club and thus gain an insight into the vast scope this field offers. Others seek social contact and find it easier through the common interest in dogs. Although I had always loved and trained dogs, I had never thought of entering competitive Obedience until I hit a bad patch in my life, and in order to take up a new interest I plunged into Obedience. My only regret is that so many years had previously elapsed before I came to know its fatal charm and fascination, which have gripped me ever since. I have a lot to thank competitive Obedience for – a husband I met at the shows, a host of friends I meet regularly each week, the thrill and excitement of competing in what must be one of the fairest of sports (and long may it continue to be so!) and, not least of all, the inner satisfaction and contentment of doing something that becomes a way of life which I share with my dogs, thus building up a far deeper understanding and mutal respect than could be made possible otherwise. Yes, we Obedience enthusiasts may be mad, but there is very clear reasoning behind our madness.

Before you take that first exciting plunge into competitive Obedience training, let me say here and now that I believe any dog of any breed or sex, if in good health and not of an obviously too advanced age, can be taught all that is required to compete, without disgrace, in the top class at an Open Obedience show.

Whoever designed the Kennel Club Obedience tests was a very wise man indeed; perhaps they were the work of many wise men. They are carefully graded and obviously an enormous amount of thought has gone into their compilation. It will be seen that there is, in fact, nothing that cannot be mastered by any breed of dog or any handler of reasonably good physical condition. Unlike the Working Trial tests, where a really high standard of stamina is required from both dog and handler, these tests can be and indeed have been mastered by quite severely handicapped people and breeds of dog ranging from Dachshunds and Papillons to Rottweilers and Airedales.

It is, however, unfair to expect a dog that is below a good standard of physical fitness to make an attempt at serious training. Unless we feel well, we do not relish the thought of work, physical or mental, and a dog feels the same as we do. If you are in any doubt, a check up with your vet will put you wise, but most people in constant touch with their dogs know full well what their state of health is. Obesity is the bane of the life of the domestic pet as it is of many sedentary humans. Correct diet, perhaps a course of balanced vitamins, plenty of exercise and fresh air, and adequate rest periods in a comfortable quiet place, should keep your dog in peak form.

Before commencing any actual training for competitive work, get straight in your mind your own attitude and the attitude of your dog. Why are you going in for this type of competitive work? Is it because you want to show that you are as good, if not better than the next man? Is it that you see your dog as a winner and want to get him right to the top? If so, I should forget the whole idea. You are in danger of treating your dog as a machine instead of flesh and blood. You will drive him to the top places maybe, but you will lose more than you gain.

The best rewards in dog training are not represented by medals and trophies, red cards and diplomas. The best reward any trainer knows is when his dog has really tried to understand and to please. If you are going in for competitive work because you love your dog, you take a pride in him *as he is*, you want to do things together with him, you want to be with him, to watch him develop his character and his intelligence, then competitive work is for you.

You will have glorious opportunities of discovering each other, of watching each other's reactions and manner of working, of appreciating how much you are developing as a team. You will be able to meet people with similar interests, with highly diverse ideas on all the finer points of training. You will be able to go to two or three shows a week if you want to, and, whatever the outcome, whatever the skill of the judge, whatever the luck of the day, you will be able to leave, happy in the thought that you and your dog were together in mind and body today for all the world to see, and look forward with eager anticipation of doing just that little bit better next time.

So much for your attitude. What about that of the dog? It is not enough that he succeeds. He must enjoy success and to enjoy it he must understand what he is doing. He must want to please and to do the job well, and perhaps most important of all, he must know at the first signs of even attempting to do the right thing that this is indeed exactly what you want. Remember Golden Rule No. 4: *In Practice, Praise the Attempt.*

Having got that established, you have now to realise that there is a great deal of difference in training a puppy and training an adult. *All Training is Based on Correction and Praise* is Golden Rule No. 5, and with a puppy it is a maximum of praise and the very minimum of correction. With an older dog that has been allowed to acquire bad habits the degree of correction has to be heightened, although it should always be followed immediately by praise as soon as the dog responds. You will appreciate, therefore, that a puppy is far easier to train and the younger you start your competition work the better will be your results.

'Ah', I can hear you saying, 'but training does not start until after they are twelve months old for the Guide Dog, the Police Dog, the Sheepdog or the Gundog'.

Well, here you see, you are quite wrong. As soon as a puppy is picked for one of these jobs, its whole life is weaned towards this end. The Guide Dog, in particular, goes to a specially trained 'puppy walker' who does not merely look after it until it reaches a suitable age for concentrated training, he or she educates that puppy to a fantastic standard. How many Obedience Champions will go through revolving doors, pass close to a flame gun, walk along the top of a rail-less promenade with a raging sea beneath? Yet every Guide Dog does this type of thing long before he starts his 'training' in earnest. The potential Police Dog, Sheepdog Trial worker and gundog are carefully kept away from any means of acquiring bad habits, for curing is much harder than prevention.

One of the main reasons why all these wonderful dogs are not taken into serious training until they are mature is that in most cases they are trained by men, who, (unlike women!) realise their limitations and know that lack of patience with an immature dog is disastrous, whereas you can sometimes get away with it with a dog that has reached its maturity. Again, no dog under the age of twelve months can take the concentrated training that is expected from these worker dogs, who are usually expected to absorb a full training course in twelve weeks.

There is little about the psychology of dogs and knowledge of what makes them tick that an old shepherd or gamekeeper does not know by instinct and, over the years, the Police and the Guide Dog organisation have come to respect this inborn canniness and have learned much from them, although they do not agree any more than I do with some of the crude methods formerly used.

It always saddens me to think how little reward a dog needs for a lifetime's work, and how frequently even this little is denied him. A decent place to sleep when the work for the day is over, a meal that is not begrudged, and a quiet fondle that says 'Thank you', is all that is asked, yet I am afraid some of the finest working dogs in the country live out their lives without even that amount of attention. Happily, for every individual who neglects his dog, there are many who do not, and the status of dogs as friends and companions, as well as working partners, has been enhanced greatly since the Police realised their worth as crime preventors and assistants in the war against crime. It is a matter of pride with the Police that their dogs should be in band-box condition, each one a valued member of the force and an equally well-loved member of his handler's family. The policy has paid off a hundredfold.

The danger with a dog kept primarily as a pet and shown in open competition is if the handler cannot take defeat. It is not the end of the world to be beaten in Obedience tests – it merely means that someone else has spent more time and energy on training his dog, and, dare I say it, is probably a very much better trainer than you anyway! It is sad, however, to see the expression on some dogs' faces when they go home after not winning. They know they have done something to upset their owners and just don't understand what. This is not confined to Obedience handlers by any means. I have seen it happen in Breed showing many times – a ridiculous situation when you come to think of it, blaming the dog for not being beautiful. It would be a bad job for some of us if our worth and our well-being depended on whether we could win a beauty contest. Some of us would go a bit hungry! The dog that has tried should have his reward and the skilful trainer sees he gets it, so that the next time he cheerfully makes the effort to win for you.

No one's life is going to depend on the Obedience competitive dog. He is not being trained to do a job of work like a professional. He is a pet, I hope, before all else, and as a pet he is with us for a great deal of the day. We might just as well then start early on getting ourselves on the same wavelength and introduce him gradually over the early months to the fun of working together. At no time should you tire any dog with work for the competition ring, least of all when he is a baby. Your aim in these early stages should be to get him to learn that being with you is tremendous fun and, if he is very good, for a treat you will teach him how to please you even more. I would also like to state emphatically at this stage that no dog should ever be punished for failure to do an exercise in competition training. As trainers, we always take the blame for our dogs' inadequacies.

The first thing for him to learn therefore is that, whenever he comes to you, *whatever* he is doing or has been doing, he gets a terrific welcome. More dogs are ruined for work by receiving a slap when they come rushing up to their handlers than anything else. Make a tremendous fuss of him, make him think you are a superman, someone he always wants to be with. You will be fortunate indeed if you ever find a human being to make a god of you, so you might as well bask in your dog's idolisation.

There is nothing worse in the show ring than a dog who is undecided about the reception it is going to get from its handler. This is particularly noticeable when you come to Class C scent, where certain dogs are always very reluctant to bring in even the right cloth because they have been harshly treated in training for bringing in the wrong one. It just serves these handlers right. You cannot rectify your own inadequacies in training by taking it out on your dog. Any mistake your dog makes in competitive Obedience is entirely your fault. Somehow, somewhere along the line you have failed in your training and you must accept the responsibility.

A smart, confident recall is the basis of all competition training, and unless you can get this you will have disappointment after disappointment. Don't worry about any polish in the early stages of training. Concentrate on getting the dog to do the actual core of the exercise, the recall. In this early exercise, for instance, the essential part is that the dog comes to you. Not that he sits straight in front of you or that he stays before you call him up. These items represent the polish. The most important part is how he reacts to your voice. As soon as you say, 'Blackie, come', does he come bouncing up to you, full of joy? Or does he merely raise his head and then continue what he is doing, perhaps hare off in the opposite direction or, far, far worse, does he come to you hesitantly with his ears back, his tail trembling uncertainly between his legs? Only the first result is any use to you. Two of the others indicate an untrained or disobedient dog. The last represents a badly trained dog, and, believe me, a badly trained dog is hopeless in Obedience work.

Perhaps it would be an appropriate opportunity to talk about the use of titbits. I am not an advocate of training by bribery. A dog should work for praise alone and if you mean sufficient to your dog he will be happy to do so. I could in fact hold a titbit in front of my bitch's nose (and have done this) whilst she is working. She is concentrating so much on my face and voice that she is completely oblivious of the tasty morsel I am offering her. This is ideal, and few dogs have the single-mindedness of purpose that she has. I have, of course, been very lucky with her, but then I did choose her with a lot of care. Sister to an International Sheepdog Champion and a descendant of one of the greatest-ever lines of sheepdog breeding, her selection was not exactly haphazard. It has not all been plain sailing, however. She was not born winning certificates – whatever some people may think.

Many trainers would not tolerate the temperaments she throws sometimes like a prima donna, flouncing about when she thinks I've lost her a point here or there, and, like every other dog, she has had to be trained gradually through the stages. It was rather fun, though, bringing her out on the dot at six months and winning at her very first show. Now, at fourteen years of age, with fourteen Obedience Championship Certificates behind her and literally hundreds of first prizes, trophies, cups, medals and mementoes of glorious wins, she is enjoying her retirement. We had the thrill at her last Cruft's appearance of a special presentation of an oil painting, donated by her many admirers – a memory I shall cherish forever.

I am very proud of Fern and her achievements, but I have just as much affection, perhaps even a whisker more, for my very naughty Danny who throws away first prizes as readily as I throw crumbs to the ducks. Somehow I have failed in my training to impress upon him the importance of the occasion. He never will take me seriously in the ring. Each dog has its own character and each has its own place in my heart. Who is to say which is the best loved? Certainly not me, but clearly distinction in the show ring is not the yardstick I use or advise anyone else to use when trying to ration out the love. The dearest dog I ever owned never went near a show ring.

All this started with titbits, if I remember. I personally would never use titbits in training. Any dog that is working *only* for food rewards has no respect for his handler, or his handler's affection, or recognition of his efforts. What happens when the dog goes into the ring or is directed to work on his own initiative? He is thinking about his titbit and not about the job in hand. An occasional tasty reward when a dog has tried extra hard to master an exercise he has been having difficulty over does not come amiss, but if you get your dog into the way of finding your spoken praise a poor substitute for a piece of chocolate, what a sorry state of affairs you are building up for yourself!

5 Beginning Competitive Work

More Golden Rules: Control by Voice, Signal and Action: Heelwork

The trouble with some handlers is that they try to teach a dog something that they have not really got clear in their own minds. It is worse than useless, for instance, in a complicated exercise like Distant Control, to start teaching the dog before you know exactly what you want and how you can best obtain it. If you are in too much of a tearing hurry to teach advanced work, your dog is never likely to absorb any of the basic steps properly.

So, Golden Rule No. 6 is: *Analyse In Your Own Mind What You Are Aiming At Before You Involve The Dog.* Sit down quietly and think hard before embarking on a programme of dog training. If somewhat vague about what you want, how on earth are you going to get the message over to a creature who doesn't even speak your language? He is not a mind reader. He does not know that you have some pipe dream of an end product.

Golden Rule No. 7 is: *Break Up Each Exercise Into Small Sections.* Suppose you are teaching Novice Recall, which means leaving the dog sitting or down, you walk ahead, about turn, face your dog, call him up. He sits in front of you and on command goes round to the heel position, sitting on your left hand side. Divide this up into (1) the sit or down; (2) the stay; (3) coming when called; (4) sitting straight in front of you; and (5) going to the heel position. Now we have five exercises, not one, and this is an elementary exercise. When you come to Class C (the highest) you could divide the exercises into twenty parts.

It does not matter if you decide to teach all five parts concurrently so long as you do not fit two pieces together until you are perfectly satisfied that the dog has mastered both. Gradually build up to the complete exercise, like doing a jigsaw. In this way, you and your dog will grow in confidence. Neither of you is attempting too much too quickly, and if, as frequently happens, something goes wrong with one part of the complete exercise, you can always go back to practise that particular section again without having to go through the entire exercise. In this way you are building up a solid foundation for your training. It is extremely bad policy, for instance, to do a dozen retrieves because a dog does a crooked sit on present, but you could cheerfully do a dozen practice sit presents without the dog even seeing a dumb-bell. He's got the retrieve part right, why bore him with needless repetition of something he can do perfectly?

Very many dogs have been made unreliable in the scent through getting a clout for mouthing the cloth on return. Correction for mouthing should have absolutely nothing to do with a scent exercise, nor the retrieve for that matter. The dog should be sitting in front of you and be given a cloth or other article he is liable to mouth. He should not associate this part of the exercise with scent or retrieve: he has merely been given a cloth and told to hold it. Then if he mouths, the appropriate steps should be taken.

Praise the Attempt (remember Golden Rule No. 4?). Don't be mean with your praise. As soon as the dog shows any sign of doing the right thing, give him plenty of indication that you are pleased with his effort. There are too many dispirited dogs in training. These unfortunate animals always get the blame for what they do wrong but rarely a 'Thank you' for trying, or even a smile for something done perfectly. If you never had a word of appreciation however hard you tried, I bet you would give up sooner or later, and so does a dog.

Golden Rule No. 8 is that: *A Dog is Not a Machine.* However well you think you have taught a dog, he is not a piece of clockwork that can be turned on and perform perfectly every time. Learn to read the signs quickly when your dog is getting fed up, and finish for the day on an easy exercise with lavish praise for doing well. Never train if you are tired or fed up, or your dog is.

Golden Rule No. 9 is: *Make Absolutely Certain Your Dog Knows When He is Working and When He is Off Duty.* It is little short of lunacy, for instance, to leave a dog tied up for half an hour with the command 'Stay', whilst you go and have a drink or something. 'Stay' means 'You are working now and you will stay in whatever position I have left you for five or ten minutes whilst I go out of your sight. You, however, are not out of my sight and as soon as you alter position I shall come back and correct you, so watch it!' If you want to leave your dog whilst you go off for a long period and cannot possibly know what he has been up to whilst you are away, don't give the dog the work command, tell him 'I won't be long' or some such similar thing which means, 'I'm going away now and you will have to remain there because I have tied you up but you can sit, lie down or stand on your head for all I care whilst I'm away. Cheerio!'

This is a very important rule to make sure that the dog knows when he is on duty and when he is off, when he is working and when you have finished an exercise. Always make a habit of releasing him from an exercise with a gay, 'Well done' or 'All right then' or something to indicate that you no longer expect him to be on duty. It is a good idea to find something the dog likes doing particularly, whether it is bouncing up and down on the spot (a favourite Border Collie trick), jumping over something or playing with the lead, and to let him do his favourite trick when he has worked well.

If there are any magic secrets about dog training, they probably lie in the next three Golden Rules, the first being No. 10: *Timing is the Key to Successful Training.* This means having the knack (which can be acquired, if not inborn) of gauging the exact moment for praise or correction, of knowing when to go on and when to stop, of 'feeling' the mood and responsiveness of the dog, of judging that a mistake is about to occur and when to step in and prevent it, of knowing just when to give encouragement and boost the confidence of a soft, submissive type of dog, and how much quiet, calm appreciation to give a boisterous, extrovert dog. Help your dog all the time. Don't let him make mistakes if you can possibly help it. The split second before the dog goes wrong is the time to correct him, not after he has made the mistake. It is too late then. Keep your commands simple – it is so much easier for you and the dog – and try to cultivate a rather high, happy tone for expressing pleasure, a low tone for grumbling.

Golden Rule No. 11 is a character-builder, for I believe that *Patience and Perseverance are the Hallmark of a Good Trainer.* Cultivate these virtues and you will go a long way towards the self discipline which is essential to reach the giddy heights in any sport. My last Golden Rule, No. 12, is something you will have to do every time you set out on a few minutes practice and every time you go into the show ring. It is: *Get Your Dog's Attention and Keep It.*

Your clothes are important in training. Have nothing flapping in the dog's face. An open jacket will push him away instead of encouraging tight and attentive work. Slim-line slacks are *in* for training, whatever Paris says; skirts are *out*, as they tend to catch the attentive dog across the eyes. Do see that your shoes are soft and low-heeled.

Something you will have to appreciate is that each person has his own methods of training. It is wrong to say that such-and-such a method is right and all others are wrong. The method that gets the maximum of happy results with the minimum of effort is obviously the best for that particular handler and dog.

I strongly advise you to go to a training club where you will get atmosphere if nothing else, and where you will find a 'public' to use as practice for when you go in the ring. The secret of gaining the best from a club, however, is to train at home and use the club only as a place to try out in public what you have thoroughly trained in private. Do not even attempt a new exercise at club. This way you will mould your dog the way you want it to go without outside interference, however kindly meant, that could ruin your dog for ever. Watch out for anything in the club that is going to harm your potential winner and sit that one out. You don't have to join in everything that is going on. If you have an excitable dog you will be laying up trouble for yourself if you join in mass work. To have one other dog working either side is not a bad thing as it teaches yours to ignore distractions and

The most important
Golden Rule of all,
No. 12: *Get Your
Dog's Attention and
Keep It*: the author
and her Bearded
Collie, Osmart
Copper Coin, bred
by Mr and Mrs K.
Osborne

concentrate on you, but few dogs can concentrate on anything when twenty others are leaping around.

One serious criticism I have against the clubs is they do tend to treat all dogs alike. Of course many methods will work for many dogs, but, and here the mistakes are made, just because a certain dog does not respond to a given way of doing something it does not mean that this dog is no good. It simply means that that particular method is no good for that particular dog and it is up to the instructor and handler to find some other approach. Unhappily their knowledge lets them down and the dog gets the blame.

To get the maximum from a club, a handler should do a great deal more watching, listening and analysing than practical work. Your dog will learn very little of any use at club, but *you* can learn a great deal. Use your common sense. Watch other people's mistakes and learn by them. Why let your own dog make mistakes when you can so easily learn by others? The place to train your dog is at home in familiar surroundings, with as little outside distraction as possible. Get an exercise perfect in the kitchen, then try it in another room, then in the garden, then in a quiet park, then in a children's playground, then take your dog to a quiet training club and let him do it with the minimum of distraction. Later on, increase distraction by going to noisier training clubs, until he can do it with the maximum of distraction. Unless your dog can do the exercise as automatically and confidentially as you manage the controls of your car, he is not ready for the show ring, any more than you are ready to be let loose on the M1 if you cannot give your whole mind to the road.

One other point I will make at this stage, train the dog you have. Never mind if you realise he will be no world-shaker. Train him, right up to Class C, even if you never show him. Don't be persuaded to get a new dog because that one's 'no good'. Whoever told you that probably is no good as an instructor, anyway. You will learn a lot from every dog you train and, if you make a lot of mistakes on the one you have now, when the time comes that you can have a new puppy and bring it up the way you want it to go, you should benefit from your past experience. The world is full of people who are sure they could get to the top with the right material. The right material is useless if you don't know how to handle it. Learn now, so that when your golden opportunity comes you will not let your golden dog down.

If you are experiencing great difficulty in training your dog, I hope you will not feel that he lacks intelligence. The reverse may well be the truth. Intelligence has little to do with trainability, in fact the more intelligent the dog the more difficult he may be, and a softer, more submissive dog may well be less intelligent. Remembering that all dog training is a partnership, if your dog's I.Q. is very high, how does yours, as his partner rate? It is a sad but very true fact that one sees countless dogs in competitive obedience several jumps ahead of their handlers, whose brains are just not capable of working so nimbly. So don't think your dog is a fool if he is not winning. Perhaps you are just not exerting *your* personality enough for him.

Like human beings dogs have different degrees of sensitivity and whereas the slightest disapproval will meet with a flood of tears from one sensitive child, it may not have the same effect at all on another. You will have to feel your way very carefully here, always erring on the side of gentleness, particularly in the early stages.

Each dog is different. It is useless to think that because you have trained one, you will be able to train the next. His reactions, his method of learning, his concentration, his awareness, his willingness to please, all will be quite different from any other dog. This is what makes dog training so interesting. We all of us, from the top handlers to the rawest beginners, make a fresh start from scratch when we take on a new dog. We must feel our way, face the fact quite fearlessly that much of our knowledge acquired painfully perhaps in the past may simply not be of use to us with our new dog.

Heelwork

Equip yourself with a suitable chain slip collar of the correct size (the rings should rest level with the two tips of the shoulder bones on the dog's chest) and check that it is on the correct way. (Hold the chain in a vertical position, the bottom ring in your left hand, the top ring in your right. Lower the right hand and let the chain slip through the ring in your left hand. The ring that you are holding in your right hand is the one to attach to the lead. Make sure that this right-hand ring is put over the top of the dog's head so that the chain tightens as soon as pressure is put on the lead, and slackens when the pressure eases.) Your lead will need to be a good leather one with a safe bolt clip.

Figure 2. The correct way to wear a slip collar. The lead is fastened to the bottom ring and the dog walks on the handler's left-hand side

Heelwork can be a most attractive exercise to watch if the dog really understands and enjoys what he is doing. It is worth sacrificing accuracy and deportment in the early stages in order to get the tail waving and the dog stepping out confidently

Before involving the dog in Heelwork, make absolutely certain what you want before training. If you go wrong yourself, you cannot apologise to the dog and say, 'Oh, I really meant to do it this way.' The dog will remember the first way you did it and then be unhappy because you are not consistent in your training.

We want the dog to walk at our side in a happy but controlled manner, his head stylishly up, turning smartly as we turn, keeping close to our left side, and when we halt we want him to sit immediately at our left side in a perfectly straight 'Sit'. It is a very good idea to have a practice on your own without the dog to get the 'feel' of this exercise. If you are not used to turning on command, call out to yourself as you go, 'Forward', 'Left Turn', 'Right Turn', 'About Turn', 'Halt'. It is surprising how difficult it can be at times to remember your left from your right, and of course hesitation on your part with a dog in training does no good at all. Make your turns smart right-angle turns, not wheels, or hairpin bends, but good, 90-degree affairs. About turns should be done on the spot, and you should then follow the line you came up.

Although I think some handlers concentrate on their footwork to the detriment of the team work of dog and handler as a whole, there is no doubt that neat and careful footwork can assist greatly in the accuracy of the team. Without becoming fanatical about it, work out the best way to execute your turns without throwing the dog and yourself off balance. Remember you can include a lot of signals to your dog in your footwork if you are consistent. Always start off with the left foot, for instance, when you are taking the dog with you such as in Heelwork. In exercises such as the Stays or the Recall where you are expecting the dog to remain behind for a time, always use the right foot to leave him. This is a signal to the dog what exercise is coming up.

When you have mastered this on your own, then work out exactly what Heelwork means to a dog. At his height and on your left-hand side, you should appreciate that in order to give the results you want, he has to walk in the somewhat uncomfortable position of turning his head upwards and towards the right. I doubt whether you would like to do this for very long and this is one good reason why Heelwork should be practised for short periods only. If you get good attention and accuracy from the dog, don't chance your arm with too much work. Sheer weariness and boredom will make him sloppy.

You will also realise, I hope, that as the dog is looking to the right, towards you, it is much easier for him to walk a straight line or one veering slightly to the right, and to execute right-handed turns and right-about turns than anything else. Most training clubs teach handlers to train their dogs initially to walk in left-handed circles and introduce them very early on to left turns and even left-about turns. In my opinion, this method is in fact teaching the dog to look away from the handler, not encouraging him to keep his attention riveted on the handler as a right-handed turn will do. The only time I advocate turning left with a new dog is if you have such as an overgrown Labrador or Boxer that is trying to sit on you (literally!) and you must get him to respect you and the lead. By bumping into him and constantly turning left, he is being urged back into the heeling position. He learns that if he strains forward he will have you crashing into him and in time he toes the line. However, with a dog whose eventual goal is Class C Heelwork, taken at all speeds off the lead and during which he must stick like a limpet to your left side, the last thing you want is a dog that looks away from you!

Until you are both really good at right turns and right-about turns, don't attempt left turns and certainly not left-about turns.

You will have a number of things to help with your Heelwork. You have the collar and lead on the dog, of course, and all exercises should be done initially on the lead; you have your voice, and you have your hands. If possible, try to get the maximum response from your dog on voice control. At first, of course, he won't know what you are wanting, and you will have to use the lead and collar and your hands to assist you, but always make sure that your voice is the main command. With the dog at your left side, the lead in your left hand, get his attention, and then give a firm but cheerful command, 'Blackie, heel' or 'Close' or whatever you are going to use, and step off with your left foot. If necessary, encourage the dog forward with a hand signal or even a short jerk on the lead. However, if your voice is attractive enough and if your dog likes you, it is unlikely he will remain still whilst you move forward. *As soon as he moves* give lavish praise and continue forward. Don't hang about. Step out, if you want to, run, but all the time encourage the dog to keep up with you.

Although in the ring the lead must be seen to be slack, in training and practice, I strongly recommend holding it rather short with little play in it. This means at the slightest inattention the slip collar will tighten on the dog, immediately fixing his attention on you again. Don't however, get into the way of holding the lead tight, for then there is no different feeling to the dog whether he is carrying out the exercise correctly or not. When he is in the correct position the collar must be loose: only when he attempts to break the correct position does the collar tighten. You will not teach the dog anything by having a constantly tight collar and physically dragging him around, any more than you will teach him anything by having the lead and collar too loose and letting him meander along in his own sweet time.

Practise the halt as a separate exercise. Don't put in more than one halt, the last one, before releasing the dog from the actual Heelwork, or you will break the flow and continuity that you must encourage in these early stages. As a completely separate exercise, start off and then halt almost immediately. Do this several times to get a quick, smart sit at your side. It is easier when practising this part to hold the lead with both hands on starting off. When you halt, say 'Sit' (voice command), raise your right hand, still holding the lead, above the dog's head, giving a short upward and backward jerk (hand signal). At the same time, release the lead from the left hand, put your left hand low on the dog's haunches (not the small of the back or the kidneys or the base of the spine) and press downwards and slightly in towards you (physical action).

When you have mastered this in a straight line, turn to the right and halt. Turn to the left and halt. About turn and halt. Do all this on the spot work, but don't connect it with Heelwork as such. I always tend to put a dog into the Sit rather than wait for him to make up his mind as I like a quick response to my commands. Later on, when the dog is progressing, put a few of these touches in the Heelwork but don't overdo it, or the dog will start hesitating or anticipating a halt or a turn. Don't worry too much about a dog that jumps up at your side whilst doing Heelwork. With time this rather attractive fault dies a natural death without correction.

Crabbing (when the dog's head and fore quarters keep the 'Heel' position but the back quarters go around at an angle) is caused by over-keenness. Here, left-handed circles are very useful. They will not spoil this dog's attention. It is because he is *too* attentive, he is actually coming round in front of you to get a better look at your face, so turning left will keep his mind more on the exercise and slightly less on your fatal charms!

Another fault is lagging. I'm sorry, but if you have a lagging dog, you have only yourself to blame. You may be a social lion at the local or at your club, but to your dog you are a crashing bore. Try a bit of silliness to cheer him up. Let him off his lead and race him up the field trying to keep him as close to your left side as possible. Act like a silly idiot, and he will love you for it. You have been much too serious about it all up to now. Give lavish praise if he keeps up with you and forget about the polish for the time being. Whatever you do, don't turn left with a lagging dog.

Crooked sits, slow sits, wide about turns, wheels, and other faults should be corrected completely separately from the main Heelwork. Quick about turns will prevent a dog working forward. Put plenty of variation into your Heelwork to keep the dog's attention. Vary the pace frequently. Warn the dog what you are going to do before you do it. Don't step off and then say, 'Heel'. Give the dog due warning about a turn, particularly an about turn, but, in practice, get out of the turn quickly. If he thinks you are not in any hurry he will take his time and the chances are the turn will be sloppy.

Don't start Heelwork too early with a puppy (five months is quite soon enough even for the keenest breeds), and never depress a dog with this exercise. Close your ears to those who try to induce you to do Heelwork ad nauseum. You will have to do this exercise off the lead in the ring but in practice use the lead ninety per cent of the time. You have no control over the dog, apart from his response to your voice, once he is off the lead. Make him so used to doing perfect Heelwork on the lead that on the few occasions he does it off the lead in the ring, he is perfect at that, too.

Advanced Stand, Sit and Down

When your dog is confined to the top class is early enough to start teaching this exercise, which is incorporated in advanced Heelwork. Even then, under no circumstances connect this with Heelwork except in the show ring. It is fatal to include this with Heelwork in practice, as it causes apprehension and anticipation of non-existent halts and positions, and builds up a tension in the dog's mind, so you have been warned!

With the dog on the lead, step forward and almost immediately say 'Down' in a very firm tone, at the same time push the dog into this position even if he is already beginning to do it. You must have immediate reaction to your command. Give a hand signal as well to help. When you have done this a few times and his reactions are swift, warn him to wait in the 'Down' position, walk round him, and then away from him, back past him and stand beside him. Release him and start all over again.

Teaching the Advanced Stand, Sit and Down entails the handler walking round, not away from, the dog

When he can do this part satisfactorily, attempt the Sit, starting off in the same way but giving the command 'Sit' and doing the actions described earlier for getting the dog to take up this position. Again when he reacts well to this, warn him to wait and walk around him, eventually walking away and back past him until you take up the heeling position. Stand at the side of him and then release him.

For the Stand, it helps to use an extra lead under the tummy of the dog, or to steady him with your hand (I do not like to see handlers using their foot under the dog in this or any other exercise), and repeat as above.

6 Further Competitive Work

Recalls: Retrieves: The Stay: Distant Control

Recalls

Nothing gives a better impression in the show ring than a fast, accurate recall. You will achieve this with a confident dog that has been skilfully trained, and it is an exercise that pays wonderful dividends for the time and patience you spend towards reaching the ideal goal.

When your puppy is with you, get him thoroughly used to his name and a reward associated with it, i.e. tickling him under the chin or whatever he likes. Accompany the name by the command 'Come', spoken in a happy tone of invitation and back away from the puppy. Most puppies react quickly and will soon come racing up to see what they are missing. If the response is not quick enough for you run away after you have called the puppy and his reflexes will insist he follows as quickly as he can.

In teaching the adult dog the recall, have him on the lead, allow him to get ahead of you and then with a firm but pleasant 'Come', give a short sharp snap rather than a jerk on the lead to start the dog moving towards you. Praise this effort as though it had been his own and he will come the rest of the way to you under his own steam. Call the dog to you often, not just when you want to put him on the lead to take him home from a walk or he will associate coming to you with having the lead put on or being shut up in his kennel. He should associate this exercise with something very pleasant, and very great care must be taken not to shake the dog's confidence. He must *never* be reprimanded when he has returned to you on command whatever crimes he has been up to on the way. This is an elementary fact of dog training that is merely common sense when you sit down and think about it, but how many times do you see a handler call a dog in, and then smack it for not picking up the dumb-bell properly! By doing so, the handler has not only failed to teach the dog to improve its retrieve, he has also taught the dog to keep clear of his hands the next time he calls him up.

The handlers who get good recalls are on good terms with their dogs. They never correct a dog that comes up to them. Whilst he is there in front of them, their dog is perfect in their eyes. Teach a dog to straighten its sit by backing away and not stopping until you can see that if you stop at that point the dog will be sitting straight. Don't allow a crooked sit to occur. Later on teach the dog to come in from the right and then from the left and straighten himself on the way. A chair placed slightly to the right and slightly in front of you will ensure the dog positions himself correctly before sitting when coming in from the right, and one placed slightly to the left and slightly forward will straighten out a left-hand recall. If you can handle a long lead this can be an invaluable aid in training a dog to straighten up. Remember it is important to get the dog to straighten himself on the way in, not as he arrives at your feet. The angle is much more difficult to negotiate the closer he is to you.

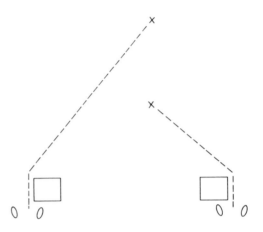

Figure 3. Correcting an angled Recall. A chair placed slightly in front and to the right of the handler will help to straighten a dog coming in from the right. Similarly a chair placed slightly in front and to the left of the handler will help to straighten a dog coming in from the left

I belong to the school of thought that believes the novice recall is the basis of all competitive training. This exercise must be perfect and is needed throughout the whole of the dog's competitive life. Class C retrieves and scent depend on a perfect novice recall to ensure that the odd half marks are not lost unnecessarily on present. Practice the novice recall, then, even though you and your dog are long out of the Novice stage and confined to the top class.

Class A recall is when the handler leaves the dog in the sit or the down position and continues forward. On the steward's command, he then calls the dog up to the heel position and both continue forward. Here again, if you are on good terms with your dog he will respond well. Never stop until after the dog has caught you up, otherwise you will encourage the dog to do a slow recall. If he is already slow, put a check cord on and give a good jerk as you call his name, run away from him so that he has got to move quickly, and follow by lavish praise as he catches you up.

The finish. When teaching the dog to go to heel, step back with the right foot and pass the lead quickly round your body, encouraging the dog tightly round behind you. If a trained dog is slack on this finish to the exercise, always go back to basic steps when necessary. Most small dogs seem to remember to keep in tightly when doing the finish if taught correctly in the first place, but many bigger dogs go quite slack and meander round in a very lackadaisical sort of way. Tighten up the dog who should know what he is doing by keeping the lead in your right hand and letting him take it round with him. He must do a tight finish under these circumstances. A dog that is learning does much better if you guide him round with the lead changing from right to left hand.

A continental finish can be taught by doing a left-about turn on the spot. This type of finish looks very smart indeed when done by a fast, neat dog, but is one to avoid unless you are absolutely sure you can do it well. It simply sits up and begs the judge to down-mark if performed lethargically and culminating with a bad sit.

Teaching the Finish. (a) The dog at the 'present' position immediately in front of the handler, ready to start the Finish

Teaching the Finish (cont.)
(*b*) On the command 'Heel' with a right-hand signal, the dog moves to go round the back of the handler's right leg

(*c*) Keeping the dog in close is the secret of a stylish Finish. Use can be made of the lead, which the dog is allowed to take round with him

The Retrieve

There is a world of difference between a puppy retrieve and a competition retrieve. The first can be encouraged at an early age if the dog shows sufficient interest, but the second must not be taught until after the puppy has finished teething (about five to six months). The puppy retrieve is not

(d) Nearly there! The handler's hands move to ensure the same tightness is achieved at the back as at the side

(e) Made it! Handler and dog congratulate each other on a good Finish. Over-eagerness has made this young Beardie put a paw on her handler's foot – a fault which should not occur if the handler stands up straight

really a retrieve at all. It is merely trying to get the puppy to pick something off the ground. See if he shows any interest at all in a suitable object like a little stick, a screwed-up ball of paper or a match box (do not use a ball or a toy which should be reserved strictly for off-duty play) and certainly don't attempt a dumb-bell at this stage. Try to get his attention on the article and then egg him on to taking it from your hand, using the command 'Hold' or 'Fetch' or whatever you intend using later on for the proper retrieve. If you do this in a corner of the room he will not be able to run off with it after he has picked it up. As soon as he takes it, show your pleasure by quietly fondling him. Try not to let him drop it, but say 'Give' and gently take it from him. This is quite enough for one training session. Try this once or twice a day and you will have instilled into him the basis of the retrieve in a play session. Be quite quick to take the article from him but don't snatch it otherwise he will grip harder if he is a bold puppy, and you will start the idea of 'mouthing' in his mind, or else you may frighten him if he is at all apprehensive and then he won't want to have anything to do with retrieving the next time. This puppy style retrieve can be started from six weeks of age onwards.

Figure 4. Different shaped dumb-bells for different purposes

Once the puppy is past the teething stage and can do a good recall, it is time to teach the competition retrieve. There is no playing about with this

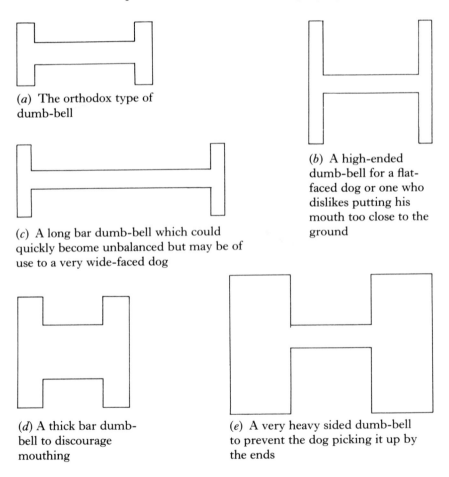

(*a*) The orthodox type of dumb-bell

(*b*) A high-ended dumb-bell for a flat-faced dog or one who dislikes putting his mouth too close to the ground

(*c*) A long bar dumb-bell which could quickly become unbalanced but may be of use to a very wide-faced dog

(*d*) A thick bar dumb-bell to discourage mouthing

(*e*) A very heavy sided dumb-bell to prevent the dog picking it up by the ends exercise to encourage bad habits. It is a serious part of competition work and should be treated as such. This does not mean, however, that it must be performed with a long face and the dog made miserable through it.

The method I am about to describe is called the 'forced' method, unfortunately, I think, as it gives people the impression that the dog is forced to do something it hates or else that the dumb-bell is rammed or 'forced' down the dog's throat! Nothing is, or rather should be, further from the truth. I hasten to point out that I am not referring to the continental forced method of twisting the dog's collar to strangulation pitch and other inexcusable brutalities, which I hope the reader of this book will regard with as much contempt as the writer of this book does.

With the 'forced' method described below, the dog understands exactly what you are trying to teach him, mouthing never arises, and if the dog drops the dumb-bell he will immediately pick it up again. Other methods tend to encourage mouthing and dropping and generally messing about.

Figure 5

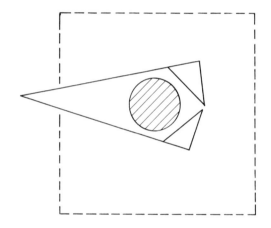

(*a*) Correct placing of dumb-bell in dog's mouth

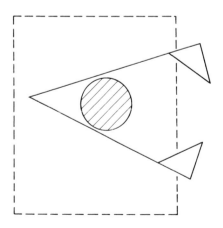

(*b*) Incorrect placing of dumb-bell in dog's mouth. Here the mouth is forced open and the automatic reaction of the dog is to eject it

Arming yourself with a suitable size dumb-bell, preferable one with square ends so that it doesn't roll all over the place, have the dog sitting in front of you. Say 'Hold' and *gently* open his mouth. Place the dumb-bell immediately behind the fangs, *not* at the back of the mouth or he will think he is choking and will try to spit it out, and do not force the thing against his front teeth if he is too quick for you and has closed his mouth again by now. Back to the beginning, open his mouth and pop the dumb-bell in, place your hand lightly over his mouth to keep it closed, repeating the command 'Hold'. As soon as you feel him take a grip on the dumb-bell, say 'Good boy, give' and immediately take the dumb-bell from him. Do this several times a

Teaching the Retrieve

(*a*) Ensure that the dumb-bell is correctly held immediately behind the 'fangs', and not thrown to the back of the mouth. The handler's hand on the end of the dumb-bell gives confidence and ensures that the dumb-bell is not dropped. The other hand is used for quiet praise

(*b*) Praise and encouragement are essential at this stage in teaching the retrieve, to ensure a firm grip without mouthing. Note how the hand remains under the chin to make an accidental drop impossible

day for several days. He will soon show signs of beginning to open his mouth when you show him the dumb-bell and give the command 'Hold'. Praise the slightest attempt he makes to do this. Once he will open his mouth to take the dumb-bell you are well on the way.

The next stage is to place the dumb-bell a few inches away from his mouth downwards towards the floor and get him to take it from here. In time hold the dumb-bell further and further away from the dog so that he has to lean forward to take it. All this will take time, depending on the dog, but it is a very sure method of teaching a reliable competition retrieve, even though it may not be the quickest method.

The Retrieve (cont.).

(c) Encouraging an inexperienced dog to lean forward to grasp the dumb-bell

(d) The 'present' of the Retrieve – a bit too close for comfort here, as Copper firmly wedges the dumb-bell between her handler's knees. Sympathetic handling of this type of over-enthusiasm at this very novice stage pays off later in the Show Ring

After a while, place the dumb-bell on the floor, but don't let go of it until the dog picks it up. Taking it from the floor without your hand there to give him confidence is a big step for some dogs and they are reluctant to do it. Persevere and you will get there in the end.

Once you have got him to this stage, call him in as in the Novice recall for a straight present, praise him quietly, take the dumb-bell and finish there. Do not send him round to heel and do not try throwing the bell at this stage. The next stage is to see if he will go further and further for the bell which you place for him each time. When he will go a short distance away from you to fetch the dumb-bell, throw it a very short distance, not more than a yard, and send him after it immediately. Do not tell him to stay before you send him. Get every part of this exercise built up well, including the sending to heel before you apply the final polish, making your dog sit at your side while you throw the dumb-bell and wait until you give him the command 'Hold'. More dogs are taught to bring in retrieve articles slowly by being nagged at to wait during the early stages of learning than anything else. The dog is a predatory animal, and his instincts urge him to chase a moving object. You can mould this instinct to your own advantage in retrieving if you are clever enough, but you will lose a lot of impetus if you take too much of the fun out of the exercise too early.

A good method of quickening up a slow retrieving dog is to go back to the stage where you throw the article and send him off immediately without making him wait for a command 'Wait', followed by the command 'Hold'.

Mouthing rarely occurs in a dog taught a 'forced' retrieve as described above. However, if the habit has already been allowed to develop, or if you think it may soon develop, the first thing to do is to make absolutely certain that the dog is actually mouthing, and if so, at what point he starts. A number of inexperienced young dogs get excited in training and pant excessively. They cannot stop panting during a retrieve and consequently the article bounces up and down in the mouth. Make absolutely certain that this is not what is happening in your case. You will put the dog back months of training and possibly never cure it of apprehension in retrieve and scent if you make a mistake and blame him for rattling of the object.

If you decide the dog is definitely mouthing, that his jaw is working on the object and it is not moving involuntarily in his mouth, make a separate exercise of sitting and holding the dumb-bell. Correct with tone of voice, and if necessary shock him into paying attention by speaking with unaccustomed severity. The shock of hearing you speak so fiercely to him will stop the mouthing. The moment he starts again, ring out your harshest tone and stop him. When he is holding it without mouthing, take it from him and praise quietly. Repeat several times a day until you feel he really appreciates what you are grumbling at. Don't return to retrieve or scent until you have cured this fault.

Like all other aspects of dog training, there are many other methods of trying to stop a dog mouthing, but I can honestly say that I have yet to see the dog that has been cured of this fault by tapping on the nose, under the chin or where have you. Tone of voice, if you can really get some venom into it, however, will do the trick. The really dedicated mouther is nearly always a tough, independent type of dog and can take quite a lot of correction of this type.

Refusing to give up the article is another trick of an independent dog. Handle as quietly as possible if he is a real gripper, but make absolutely certain he understands you are annoyed. Get him by the scruff of the neck (use gloves if he is really determined) and take the article from him. Then give it straight back to him and tell him to 'Hold'. Then tell him to 'Give' and repeat the process. This is a serious fault with the rather spoilt type of dog, or one that has been teased unfairly. Twisting the article out of the mouth of this dog does no good at all. You are not teaching the dog anything except to grip tighter next time. You must go right back to the elementary stage of teaching the dog the meaning of 'Hold' and 'Give'.

The Stays – Stand, Sit and Down

The Stays are very important exercises, not only in their own right, but also as a basis for Distant Control. I teach the Stays very early indeed and I teach Distant Control very late indeed. The reason for this is that the dog which has been taught D.C. too early is often unreliable on the Stays. A dog's mind closely connects these two exercises, and it cannot readily distinguish between them unless it has been given the chance to absorb the Stays very thoroughly long before it starts to learn D.C. However, you can save yourself a great deal of work for future D.C. if you bear the close connection in your mind. The secret it not to let the dog associate the two exercises.

It is easy enough to teach the average dog to Stand, to Sit and to Down, and to stay in those positions, and I will run through the exercises with you in a moment, but it is *how* you teach them which will either help or hinder you when you want to start D.C. If you make a habit of always placing the dog in the position you want him to do and not allow him to do it himself, you can ensure that he always moves the way you want him to go and not the way he may naturally want to go himself. Most dogs will move forward, for instance, when they do the Sit or the Down or the Stand, and most handlers let them. If, however, you make your dog move backwards every time it takes up the Stay position, it is practising, although it doesn't know it, for a really spot-on D.C.

The Stand: teach this very early. It is so much easier to handle a small puppy than an adult dog and they don't get offended in the same way that some adults, particularly male, seem to do if handled too much. Teach

A superb
temperament.
Champion Seaanca
of Perryhow, bred by
Mona Bennett, has
the superb
temperament of all
good
Newfoundlands.
She's our gentle
giant!

from the Sit position, moving the back legs backwards with your hand and
not allowing the front legs to come forward. The dog's natural method of
standing is to move the front legs but, as explained above, if you always
place your dog in the Class B Stand he will get up the way you want him to
go, and this habit will develop throughout his early competitive life until he
will automatically (we hope!) do it in D.C.

You will have to teach your dog to stand steadily and confidently for the
Temperament Test in Novice and Class A. Remember this is not supposed
to be a Stand for Examination, nor a Stay Test, and there is nothing in the
Regulations to indicate a loss of marks if your dog moves a little in this
particular exercise.

To avoid confusion in the dog's mind between the Class B Stand and the stand in the Temperament Test, use completely different commands for the two exercises. The judge will expect to be able to handle your dog without undue resentment. He will want to run his hand down the dog's back without losing a finger and, in fact, won't want much reaction at all. You will have to dicourage the tendency to sit by training against it. Use your special command such as 'Keep steady' or something similar and practise keeping him in a stand whenever he hears the command and someone else touches his back. This is quite easy – breed show dogs do it all the time and any dog trained for the beauty show ring would walk this part of the Obedience Class.

Teaching the Stand. Reassure the dog each time in this exercise

Teaching the Sit.
The author uses all
the 'aids' to assist her
German Shepherd
Dog, Seaanca
Plasmajor Donna u.
Blitz

The Sit : supporting your puppy's head under the chin, command him to Sit and at the same time gently assist him backward into this position. A great deal of praise follows and you release him by saying, 'All right' or 'Well done' or something to let him know that you do not expect him to remain in that position any longer. Do not use force with pushing your puppy into the Sit, and do not concern yourself with untidiness at this stage. His bones are still soft and you can do quite a lot of damage to his hips if you push him around too much. Gentle assistance with your hands is all that is required. Your puppy will soon catch on and will respond happily.

The Down : I teach the Down in a very easy way. All I do is say 'Down' when the puppy is already down, and merely explain to him what he is doing. You must be extra gentle with puppies and young dogs in this exercise as they can quite easily get upset over it. If the puppy is standing, push from the shoulders backwards into the Down position. If he is sitting, again push against the shoulders, moving him slightly backwards if you can. Adults need firmer handling, but keep your face well away from an adult dog you are pushing into the Down. Some of them can turn rather nasty. The reason is that the dog, particularly the male dog, feels at a disadvantage in the prone position and he will sometimes resist quite strongly to avoid getting into it. Lift the difficult dog's left foot and push on his right shoulder. This method should take him off balance.

Teaching a dog to stay

At first, stay beside your dog and release after a very few seconds. Increase the length of time before you release. Stand in front of the dog and then move back to the heel position. Walk round the dog and back to heel position. Walk a foot away from the dog and wait, then move back. Increase the distance and the time, but do not be tempted to go out of sight until you are absolutely certain the dog is steady. Don't forget, either, to give the dog a clear and firm command every time you want him to do this exercise. Repeat the command frequently in the early stages. Help him to understand what you want. Don't leave him unsure of what he is supposed to be doing.

The first few times you go out of sight, nip smartly behind a post or a tree and out the other side before the dog realises that you have in fact gone out of sight. Again, very, very gradually increase the length of time you are out of his sight. A good idea is to leave the dog in the garden and go out of sight in the house or a shed so you can see him through the window while he cannot see you. You can then correct him immediately he defaults. It is useless leaving a dog in the Sit, going out of sight for two minutes and on finding the dog down on return, correcting him. He needs correcting the second he goes down, not thirty seconds later. Never practise the Down immediately following the Sit, although you will most likely have to do them in this order at a Show.

Teaching the Down. Peter Mulvany praises the dog as it takes up the correct position. Note how the handler keeps at the side of the dog to create confidence

The Sit Stay, with Fern, Danny, Tara (Seaanca Solitaire) and Dell, all well-known winners at Championship Shows

Always release the dog from one position and get him up on his feet before taking up the second position when doing the Stays one after another at a Show or in class, otherwise he may anticipate your command and take up the second position as you return to him for the finish of the first. A dog that comes out of the Stays is usually inexperienced, however old it is and whatever the handler says! A dog that alters position has frequently been poorly trained.

Distant Control

You will never appreciate the truth of Golden Rule No. 1 *Prevention is Better Than Cure* more than the day you start teaching Distant Control, the exercise in competitive obedience which shows perhaps more than any other exactly how much control you have over the dog. If you have trained your dog from puppyhood to move into position correctly, i.e. backwards, and not forward as his natural inclinations dictate, you will have taken the hard work out of this exercise. The whole idea is, in fact, that the dog

should not move more than its length in any direction whilst performing six alterations of position.

It is quite simple to train any dog to do the six positions on command so long as you don't have to worry about where he ends up, but to do them on the spot, which is what we must aim at, is a different matter altogether.

The first and probably the most important thing to remember when teaching, and later when practising, this exercise is that although it is called Distant Control, it should be done one hundred per cent of the time when learning and seventy-five per cent of the time after learning either at the side of the dog or in front of him, very close to. I prefer to train initially at the side of the dog because you have better vision of what he is doing with his individual feet from the side, and gradually move round to the front when I am absolutely sure he is doing it perfectly. Do not move away from your position almost on top of the dog until you have trained for weeks and possibly months, and know that he can do each change of position perfectly. In practice, go right back to this training technique for most of the time, gradually inching your way back from the dog until at last you can do the exercise perfectly twenty-five yards away.

The Down Stay

It is a good tip to leave reasonably long gaps between the positions. Many dogs anticipate the change in position and it is frustrating to lose points unnecessarily on any exercise. Distant Control is something a dog needs reminding of quite often, particularly when learning or having just learnt.

If your dog has been accustomed to being handled in the Stay exercises he will respond readily to the change of positions in Distant Control. It is only by constant repetition that this exercise can then be perfected. There are various methods of moving the dog, some people use their feet – a habit I dislike intensely – others use the lead, some have a body strap around the dog, but hands seem as good as anything else and, in my opinion, the most reliable. Exaggerate the backward movement in training. The dog will not go back nearly as much in the ring and you are merely instilling in him the importance of moving backward rather than forward.

Do not practise Distant Control or Advance Stand, Sit and Down on concrete or hard floors. A dog can easily chip its elbow, resulting in a searing pain that lasts for years, and you will never get D.C. out of a dog with chipped elbows. Always choose a grassy field or a wooden floor or a piece of carpet, so that there is no chance of injuring or frightening the dog.

From the Down or the Sit, then, lift the dog backwards into the Stand, ensuring that the back feet, not the front, move. From the Stand to the Down, push the dog's shoulders downwards and backwards. From the Down or Stand to the Sit, walk into the dog, pushing it backwards. From the Sit to the Down, allow the dog to come its natural length, but not an inch over.

Although you are sure your dog can do the exercise perfectly when you are near, you will probably experience difficulty with him in the show ring. Practise the exercise at home or at class with the dog on the edge of a stage or a platform so that he can't come forward, or at the top of your stairs or on a table. Another method is tying the dog by a short lead to something to prevent him from coming forward, or putting an obstacle in the way like a low rope that he must not step over. You will have to try by trial and not too much error, I hope, to see which method works best for your own dog. However, if taught correctly in the first place, there really should be little call for all these extra 'aids'.

7 Sendaway, Jumping and Agility

Redirection: Box Training: Importance of Fitness in Jumping: Agility tests

The Sendaway is a complicated exercise to teach, probably because it is so easy to cause the maximum confusion to the dog. Up to this point, we have concentrated on gaining immediate response to our voice; we have encouraged our dog to look up to us (literally at least!) and we have taught him that when he comes towards us he is the greatest. Now we want to reverse all that, and, unless he moves away from us, we are going to be disappointed.

Look at all this from the dog's point of view. In an exercise like the retrieve where he must leave us, he has grown accustomed, through careful training, to know that there is a purpose in leaving our side. He goes out to fetch something for us and receives our warm thanks on return. But what about the average dog being sent out on the Sendaway? The poor thing generally has little or no idea what the exercise is about, and the handler has failed miserably to point out to him any meaning behind it all. Because the exercise has not been broken into small sections in training and each section perfected before it is joined to the next, there is nothing to fall back on and to build up again on a solid foundation when things go wrong, and the poor old dog, given a harsh command 'Go', which sounds suspiciously like the negative 'No', and a vague hand signal pointing away from his beloved master, is supposed to know by instinct that he is to travel in a straight line away from his handler in a direction which has previously been indicated by the judge, until told to drop and later recalled to his handler.

Well, of course, the dog doesn't know anything at all about these rules and regulations, and so we see dog after dog, even quite experienced B and C dogs, looking most unhappy when it comes to the Sendaway exercise simply because they really don't know what is expected of them. For some reason unknown to them, their handlers want them to leave them, assisted on the way, if they dare to stop and glance round for further instructions, by a scowl and a glare, a hand raised indignantly and a repeated command of that horrid 'Go'.

The first essential, then, is to make up your mind that it is possible for your dog to enjoy the Sendaway exercise just as much as he has enjoyed learning the other exercises so far. It all depends on the method of teaching. I believe that to enjoy it, the dog must understand exactly what it is you want, so that he knows when he is going right and when he is going wrong. In order to convey all this complicated matter to a creature who doesn't speak your language, it is important that you do a lot of brain work before you involve the dog.

As you will realise from the above description of the way many dogs perform the Sendaway at shows, their owners' teaching methods, such as they are, are hopeless, and if a decent Sendaway results, it is pure chance. What you must do to cut down chance is to convey to the dog that there is something out there that you want him to make for and to keep going straight for it until you say the magic word 'Down', which means he has found it. I do not advocate box training with a new dog, although I know a lot of people will disagree with me here. Box training means putting down a taped box one yard square or four cones about a yard apart and sending the dog to it. This is the type of thing you will get at a number of shows, but, in my opinion, it teaches an inexperienced dog always to expect something like this to make for and he consequently is not doing a Sendaway as I understand it – which is going in a straight line until told to Down, and also he is liable to come unstuck at a number of outdoor shows when the judge has only very small markers, visible in the long grass to the handler, but not to the dog. A few occasions of failing to find this 'box', as he has been taught to look for, and his confidence goes completely, whereas the dog that is not initially box trained accepts the situation and takes it all in his stride. Later on, when the dog is completely confident of leaving your side and continuing forward until told to drop, is the time to introduce him to various types of boxes, tapes, sticks, posts, cones, squares, etc. and to try and neaten him up so that he realises if he does see this type of obvious set up he is to make for it.

How, then, do you start to teach the Sendaway? Like everything else in this book, I believe you do it by gradually building up various sections and then fitting them together like a jigsaw. You make it easy and pleasant for the dog to do it right. You don't want him to go wrong, and if he does, it is your fault. You go back several steps every time there is a mistake, for you have to correct and this is something you want to avoid. So keep it simple.

Later on, at the shows, I strongly advise that you accept the Sendaway the dog does, and do not try to redirect him unless you know your dog sufficiently well and have not only taught him a good redirection as a separate exercise but also know that he does not get upset by redirection. Many dogs, unless taught redirection extremely carefully, are made unhappy by it and it spoils their next Sendaway at another show. It is simply not worth the risk. After all, once the dog has gone wrong you have lost enough points to miss the top places, so why not accept the fact instead of risking upsetting the dog for next week's show.

An experienced dog will go wrong on the Sendaway for many reasons, the most usual being (1) you have set him up wrong, and (2) a box trained dog has caught sight of something you hadn't noticed, i.e. a sweet paper, a clump of buttercups, different shading and texture of grass, a bald patch of earth, a tree or a handbag in the far distance, and he thinks that is the box. As both these eventualities can hardly be classed as disobedience on the part of the dog, you will be better off letting him think he is right and downing him where he goes, than waving your arms around and shouting your disapproval at him.

The first step in teaching my Sendaway is to make sure you have an immediate drop on command. Practise this as explained for the Down position in Advanced Stand, Sit and Down until you have only to shout Down and it is as though a string had been pulled and the dog's legs collapse from under him. The next stage is to realise that until he knows what is wanted in a 6-in. Sendaway he cannot be expected to increase the distance and do the exercise with any confidence or accuracy. Therefore in these early stages you must indicate to him that there is something that you want him to go to. If you can get him to go a matter of 12 in. and know what he is doing, he will go a hundred yards with confidence.

The method I use is back to front from the more orthodox ways as I increase the distance myself and do not expect the dog to increase it. I will explain. I always send a dog to a wall, a hedge, a line of chairs, a background of some sort and get him used to going right up to it. Many dogs will not go the distance because they have not been trained to go up to a barrier. All their training has taken place in the middle of a field or a garden, and it does not occur to them that they have to continue until they can go no further. This early training habit of going as far as he can is particularly important for the Working Trial dog, who certainly must not decide for himself when he has gone far enough until he can literally go no further. The Sendaways in Trials are considerably longer than those in Obedience shows.

It is a good idea in the early stages to use something heavily impregnated with your scent, i.e. an old jacket or cardigan as a Sendaway target. Place this close to the wall or hedge. Pat it and make a fuss of it and put the dog down on it, giving first your command 'Away' or 'Straight' or 'Go'. Neither of these last two words are particularly recommended as they sound too much like 'Wait' and 'No'. 'Away' is a good word because it is unlike any other used in training and it is pleasant sounding, not cross like 'Go'. Praise the dog when down on the target and release him. Repeat the process two or three times.

Now try to get him to move a matter of inches to the jacket. Have him on the lead and lean forward as though to go with him. As he grasps what you want, increase the distance until he will go forward with you a few yards. Each time he does it, go up to him and praise him before releasing him.

When he will do this off the lead, do not call him back from the target until you are ready to do a proper recall as for Class A. By calling him back to you from the starting position you are teaching him the very bad habit of jumping up out of the box immediately he has done a good Sendaway, so as to get your praise. You must go up to him to praise him in the correct position before releasing him. When you are satisfied with this, roll up the jacket to make it seem smaller and send again. Eventually take up the jacket and send the dog to the spot where the jacket has been. You will now be getting a good straight Sendaway to nothing. Don't run before you can walk, however, and when you want to choose a new site for your Sendaway go back to square one with the jacket drill. Eventually the penny will drop and you will be able to send the dog in any direction to nothing. You will appreciate now what I said earlier on about this method being a sort of back to front method of teaching the Sendaway. You are not doing what most people do, increasing the distance by sending the dog on, you are building up his confidence by sending him to the same place, and the same time increasing the distance by moving back yourself. His confidence must increase because he is always right to go back to the familiar spot. The other method makes the dog worry because he is never apparently right. If he returns to the spot he went to before he is immediately told to go on. He feels you are never satisfied with his efforts.

Never be afraid to go back several stages when practising Sendaway. Run up with a nervous dog who has gone rusty on this exercise and treat him like a novice to increase his confidence.

Somewhere during the training programme you must teach him to wait for the command 'Away' before he leaves your side. However, I am not one of those who believe anticipation the greatest crime in the dog calendar. I would much rather see a happy, confident performance by a keen, eager dog who cannot wait to show off, than a miserable performance from a

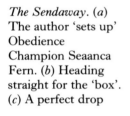

The Sendaway. (a) The author 'sets up' Obedience Champion Seaanca Fern. *(b)* Heading straight for the 'box'. *(c)* A perfect drop

depressed creature who is only too thankful to sit by his handler's side and hope in vain that the dreaded command to 'Go' will never be uttered. Obviously the polish must come eventually or you will lose valuable marks, but in the early training take a tip from the wise old shepherds who say, 'Any fool can stop a dog. It takes an expert to make it go again'.

There are various methods of keeping a dog straight once it has caught on to the idea of the Sendaway. Some trainers are great believers in long tapes set a yard apart. The idea is to send the dog up the middle and he will go straight rather than cross the tapes. I'm afraid you see the results of this when the dogs so trained run up the side of the roped rings at outdoor shows instead of staying towards the centre of the ring. If you do use this method, for heaven's sake be sensible about it and use thin black tapes or fine wire so that they are practically invisible to the dog.

Another very good method which you can use if you live in the North on one of those estates which have 'alleys' or narrow passages between terraces of houses is to send the dog up these. It is impossible for him to go wrong. Another method is to use the sunray style paths you sometimes find in public parks. But remember all these methods are building up an association in the dog's mind that may prove undesirable. True you are making him go straight but only because he has no choice. Try to reproduce the situation as it will be in the ring and you will have more chance of him going right on the day.

Later on you will have to box train your dog although I believe in winning my Class Bs with dogs that have not been box trained. However in Championship C it is necessary to have a dog that recognises the weird and wonderful arrangements that emerge from the fertile imaginations of some of our judges. When starting to box train, use a very obvious box that the dog can hardly miss. Make him go in the front of the box and aim for the back. To cure going in the side you will have to do very short Sendaways and get them right before increasing the distance. If your dog is slow in dropping, run up behind him and pounce as you shout 'Down'. Don't always do the same recall or the dog will anticipate. If he is slow at responding to the recall, run away from him as you call. Frequently go up to the keen dog and praise him in the box, tell him to wait and do a recall after a fair pause. Don't let him anticipate if you can possibly help it, but don't make the mistake of telling him off if he does or he will think he has gone wrong on the actual Sendaway. You have already instilled the idea of target boxes in the dog if you have trained the way I advise and it is a comparatively simple matter to get a dog to drop on a small card or piece of paper in readiness for the very small target boxes that some judges favour.

The best Sendaway dogs of all will sit and concentrate on a spot thirty yards away. On command they will go in a straight line to nothing and keep going until told to drop. Unfortunately box training spoils many dogs for this perfect type of Sendaway.

Teach your dog to cross white lines on the way to the Sendaway box, as many indoor venues are marked up for games courts and have these distractions on the floor. White lines will not worry your dog until he is box trained. Once he is box trained everything he thinks could be interpreted as a box will tend to worry him.

The setting up of the dog is important. Some dogs dislike a lot of handling and frankly I think it is quite unnecessary to pull the dog about in the way you often see at the shows. Make sure the dog is concentrating in the direction you want him to go. Get behind him and see his back is straight. See his head is pointing in the right direction. If it isn't cup your hands over his face so that he is looking down his nose. Point out to the dog the direction you want him to take and, if you are clever enough and have taught the dog to pick out various landmarks, tell him you want him to make for a point on the horizon that is in a direct line with the box.

Redirection

If you want to teach redirection, do so as an exercise completely separate from Sendaway. Do this tight up against a wall or a hedge. With the dog on a line, say 'Right', indicate with your right arm and move the dog over flush with the wall to the right. Until he will move towards the right with confidence on command, do not attempt to teach him to move to the left. When you teach him to move left, say 'Left', indicate with your left arm and move the dog again flush with the wall to the left. After he has learned this exercise never move the dog in both directions on the same day. Obviously a sheepdog must move freely in either direction when working sheep, but he sees the *results* of his movements. To the Obedience trained dog there is no obvious result, and you will get a much quicker and cleaner response to your command if you do your redirection right one day and left the next.

Jumping

The most important thing to ensure before jumping your dog is that he is fit and physically capable of doing the work you set him. If you are in any doubt, consult your veterinary surgeon and ask him to check heart, etc., and to advise you whether or not to go ahead with this side of training. It is grossly unfair to make a dog jump if he is unwell or incapable of achieving the heights required by the Working Trial regulations, i.e. 3-ft hurdle, 9-ft long jump, 6-ft scale.

As you are no doubt aware, certain people are built for sport and others clearly are not, and it is the same with dogs. Equally, the people who are capable physically of running a mile or pole-vaulting enjoy this type of activity, and from an early age will seek opportunities to improve their skill and physique. It is very similar with dogs. Some find enormous pleasure in jumping over the breakwaters on the beach or bouncing about on the spot. These are the dogs to train for Working Trial jumps. They love it and will respond happily to training. Some dogs, notably Greyhounds and Afghans, are veritable canine athletes and if you can persuade them to do the rest of the Trial test you should sail through your qualifications. Certainly the jumps will present no difficulty. The long legs of these dogs will almost stride over the obstacles.

To expect a tiny dog, or a heavily built animal with little spring in its hind-quarters who has never shown any inclination to want to jump over the smallest barricade, to attempt the heights necessary amounts to cruelty, and I am very much against ambitious owners urging their dogs, particularly in the scale, to attempt heights completely beyond their capabilities. It is extremely unfortunate in my opinion that the Kennel Club Working Trials include the compulsory scale. While few dogs of reasonable health and stamina find difficulty with the hurdle and the long jump, the scale is a different proposition altogether, and I would like to see this potentially dangerous and completely pointless exercise dropped from the tests. It proves nothing except that the dog is big enough and built strongly enough to do it. As far as I can see it has nothing to do with willingness or skill and bars a large number of otherwise superb dogs from even entering the Working Trials.

If you have decided that your dog is fit enough and capable physically of successfully tackling the scale, I strongly advise you to take these precautions. Always inspect the jump back and front before sending the dog over it. A broken bottle, a rusty nail or some other hazard could finish your dog's career. A loose board or a rickety jump will mean hard work to persuade him to get over the next time. To make life more pleasant for the scaling dog, tack a sack over the top, and put a couple of old mattresses on the landing side so that he does not constantly jar his shoulders. A scale with footholds is very much easier to negotiate and I see no reason why your home ground scale should not have this assistance in training.

Jumping is physically very tiring and once the dog is trained and in competition a weekly practice jumping session should be sufficient. In training, three attempts at any one jump are ample and the dog should be jumped daily until he is reaching near maximum height, then the jumping session should be dropped to two or three times a week.

The best background training you can do to prepare your dog for maximum efforts is to build up his road work and increase his free running periods. There is no substitute for this for any kind of athlete, human or canine. Footballers have to do it, runners have to do it, boxers, jumpers, all have to put in their footslogging, and it is exactly the same with horses and with dogs. Muscle can be built up gradually and strengthened wonderfully – entirely by roadwork. Do not run the dog, and do not expect to get away with it lightly yourself by cycling with the dog. This tends to overbuild some muscles and strain others, and you will defeat your own object. A brisk walk is the answer, as fast as you can go but never letting the dog break into a trot. If you do this religiously every day you and your dog will be fit for anything, and even if your dog can't manage the 6-ft scale, I bet you will be able to! Free running in country surroundings, relaxes the dog mentally while strengthening physically, and this side of his routine should never be neglected.

The Hurdle: the easiest jump to start on is the Hurdle. Put it very low (about 1 ft) and with the dog on the lead and a leather collar (never jump a dog in a chain collar) go with the dog, and together you and the dog jump over it. Give the command 'Jump' or 'Over' in an excited tone just as you take off. Do this until the dog will jump over on its own without the lead and with you running up to a point level with the jump but not going beyond it. Gradually increase the height of the jump by 6 in. each time until the dog is clearing 3 ft easily.

The Hurdle. Donna

The Long Jump: the long jump is best tackled by putting the jumps together at first to make a 3 ft 6 in. spread. Show the dog the length of the jump, otherwise he will tend to jump high and land in the middle of it. Again go with him on the lead and jump with him. When he will do this on his own with you stopping short of the jump, encourage him to get in the habit of dropping into the Down following the jump and waiting for you to meet up with him to release him. Gradually increase the length of the jump until the dog is clearing 7 ft 6 in. You will now probably experience a spot of difficulty getting him to achieve the full 9 ft. One tip is to put a small 1 ft hurdle in the middle of the long jump at about 6 ft to 7 ft 6 in. This will make the dog jump the height that he must make to go a greater distance. Once he is clearing 7 ft 6 in. well, he will be ready to increase the length of the jump and you can dispense with the hurdle unless you get stuck again, in which case return to the 7-ft length and build up to 8 ft with the hurdle.

The Long Jump.
Clough (Seaanca
Osmart Black Gold),
a Bearded Collie

The Scale: in teaching the scale jump you must insist from the start that the dog returns back over the scale. Again on the lead, take the dog over a very low scale (approximately 2 ft 6 in.) that he can easily jump, just to get him used to going over and back. Once he will do this without the lead, and perhaps without you having to go over with him, raise the scale to a height that he cannot possibly clear jump. This is important, because he will injure himself badly if he tries to clear jump and lands on top of a rigid scale jump. So raise it up to at least 4 ft 6 in. or more. Stagger the slats of the jump to make things easier and do everything you can to encourage him to scramble up the jump. Stand behind him and if he misses the jump catch him and don't let him fall back. If you can manage it, lift him to the top of the jump and hook him on by the front feet. Give him a slight shove and he will be able to haul himself to the top. Then let him land the other side. As soon as he has landed, run round the other side and send him back over. If he is a willing and able jumper he will soon catch on to the idea – so long as you don't let him fall – and he will grow to enjoy it and the sense of achievement it gives him. It is only a matter of time and experience before he will be doing the full height. You will then have to train him to wait in either the Stand, Sit or Down position until recalled over the scale. The Stand or the Sit are recommended, not the Down.

The Scale. Dell

Do remember these important points when scaling a dog. It is easy for a dog to injure himself on the scale jump and you should do everything you can to avoid this. If you stand close to the jump as the dog takes off you will be in a position to catch him and avoid having him fall back at a missed jump. This is very important in training and in practice, for if the dog is discouraged by too much failure he will be reluctant to try again. You have to let him take his chance at Trials but there is no need to in practice, so help him all you can. A dog thrives on encouragement in this exercise above all, so show your admiration in no uncertain manner at his achievements and at his efforts.

Agility

Agility tests have recently come to the fore as a competitive form of dog training. The Kennel Club regulations for agility tests S(5) (see Appendix) state:

'Agility tests are considered to be a "fun" type competition designed for spectator appeal.'

However, success in these as in any other form of training requires dedication and practice. Enthusiasm from both dog and handler are very much the case for success, and the dog's enthusiasm can easily be destroyed by either badly constructed obstacles, or by bad training.

The Kennel Club list 12 approved obstacles, though course builders may submit others for approval if desired. We will consider the approved obstacles here.

Several of the obstacles can be related to the jumping discussed earlier, namely the hurdle, the brush fence, the A Ramp and the long jump. Remember start your training small and build up to the required sizes, give your dog confidence. The table and the pause box can also be related to earlier work, particularly the advanced stand, sit and down.

So let's consider the more unusual obstacles. The dog walk, height 4 ft 0 in minimum, 4 ft 6 in maximum. Walk plank, width 8 in minimum, 12 in maximum. Length 12 ft 0 in minimum, 14 ft 0 in maximum. These are the Kennel Club approved dimensions. But in training, remember build up your dog's confidence. Make sure your board is thick enough to take his weight without undue flexing. Stand at ground level and build up in 3 or 6 in steps to that 4 ft 0 in minimum. Get your dog going confidently at every height before you increase to the next. The see-saw. The beam for this has the same limits in dimensions as the beam in the dog walk. So in training it makes sense to use the same beam. Make sure your pivot point is firmly fixed and that the axis point moves freely, build your see-saw so that you can increase the height of the central pivot in stages to that 2 ft 3 in maximum. Again go steadily, don't frighten your dog by starting at the maximum height, build up and let his confidence develop.

Remember the construction of your training obstacles can make or break your dog's confidence, take care with them.

Again relating obstacles we come to the Hoop, the Pipe Tunnel, and the collapsible Tunnel.

The hoop is probably one of the easiest obstacles to train for, as your dog should enjoy jumping or else you are wasting your time in agility tests. Start with a hand held hoop at ground level, gradually raising it from the ground, before mounting it on an appropriate stand.

For the pipe tunnel, if you can, I would advise plastic water butts with the ends cut off for training, you can build up lengths to give you the overall maximum, but make sure that you fix each section firmly, so that it cannot move when the dog is going through, or his confidence will go. Start with your hoop, then a quarter water butt section, then a half water butt, building up your tunnel length in sections to the full 12 feet.

The collapsible tunnel is one of the more difficult obstacles. My advice is start as for the tunnel with your hoop, extend from this a second hoop with your flexible tube attached, and I would suggest you use the maximum allowed diameter of hoop. Do not let the tube collapse yet, hold it externally by wire overhoops. When you get to the full 12 foot length, and your dog will go confidently through this non-rigid tube, then start to allow the last section to sag from the outer supports. Do it in stages until it is finally touching the ground and your dog has gone confidently through every stage. Then steadily working from the last section forward collapse the tube bit by bit until you have your full collapsible tube. Remember your dog's confidence, so don't rush it.

We come now to the Weaving poles.

For training I suggest you use the 2 ft maximum distance between poles as your standard but to start, it does not matter how wide you go, you have to convey to your dog exactly what you want. So initially on the lead with poles up to 4 ft apart, you can get your dog going, then reduce the gap, to your 2 ft standard, as you go on.

In agility tests we want speed more than accuracy, speed needs a happy, confident dog. Confidence is built by good, patient training.

8 Nosework and its Problems

The Dog's Natural Ability: The Human Element: Training for
Competition

Now we come to what for me is the most fascinating and rewarding part of
dog training – nosework. It is fascinating because it is the one thing we can
be absolutely certain the dog knows a great deal more about than we do.
For this reason alone it is absolutely essential never to reprimand the dog
for 'failing' scent, unless we are completely positive that we are right and he
is wrong. But we can never be really sure, even when we have prepared the
cloths ourselves, for this is an exercise we cannot check for accuracy, and
we must always give the dog the benefit of the doubt. If we have not
supervised the preparation of the cloths personally, we are guilty of a very
serious training error if we show annoyance when the dog 'fails' scent.

Unfortunately in the past some judges had no idea of preparing scent.
Happily nowadays the Kennel Club have adopted my suggestion that all
blanks and decoy cloths should be prepared by the Show Executive,
independent of the judge, so there should be fewer scent 'failures',
unhappy handlers, and thoroughly confused dogs.

It is no use whatsoever thinking, that because you have given your cloths
a good wash, hung them up to dry in the wind and then ironed them into
neat little squares that your scent is no longer with them. Your scent is on
those cloths even more than when you started, and it will take about twenty
years for it to leave them! The only way to be sure your scent is not on a
cloth is for someone else to cut them up from his own material and you
must not handle them in any way or leave them around where your scent is
heavy, e.g. in your house or car. Scent is quite daunting. It hangs around
for years, and just because we cannot 'do' scent, we tend to get careless
about it and then blame our dogs when they get confused. If you want to try
a little experiment, get someone to slip on an old sweater of yours that you
haven't worn for ages and have been meaning to throw out. Watch the
expression on your dog's face when he gets your scent from someone else!

Some judges used to bring all their own cloths to the show, take the
'scented' cloths, the decoys and the blanks out of the same polythene bag
which had been brought to the show in their own car, and think they were
giving the dogs a fair test. Unfortunately every single one of those cloths
carried his scent and the better scenter the dog the more likely he was to
'fail' that particular judge's scent. All that happened was that the blanks
went down as cold scent of the judge, the correct cloth and the decoys went

down as the hot scent of the judge. All the decoy steward did when he 'scented' the cloth was to warm up the original scent. You can do the same just as effectively by putting the cloths on a radiator to warm up.

One very effective way of 'cheating' a dog, intentionally or not, is to use what are called 'tailor's cloths' – I have renamed them 'failers's cloths'. These are small sample squares of suit materials. Each type of material has its own scent. One wood does not smell the same as another. (Try burning a log of apple tree and then a piece of pine). Neither does a cloth material such as serge smell the same as terylene. If you want to make sure a dog fails scent, all you have to do is to put down a piece of serge which a decoy has 'scented', which in actual fact means warmed up, bringing out the heavy serge smell which will stifle any fainter human scent. You, in turn, hot up another piece of serge and a piece of terylene. The terylene goes down as your scent and the dog is given the piece of serge. Unless the dog is used to being tricked in this way or lucky enough to hit the terylene first, he will almost invariably bring in the serge with the 'decoy' scent on it. Even if he does hit the terylene cloth first with your scent on it, it is unlikely that he will do more than hesitate over it. The serge smell is so strong that he is in actual fact trying to match up the scent of the material rather than the fainter human scent.

In a more subtle way, a dog can be cheated by using a mixture of natural fibres, such as wool or cotton, and man-made fibres, such as nylon. There are many possibilities. Obviously when this type of situation happens in the show ring it is done through sheer ignorance on the part of the judge, but unfortunately whether meant or not, the marks come off when the dog 'fails' and, worse still, the handler blames the dog and the dog loses confidence in what he knows is right. *Never*, therefore, blame your dog for failing Class C scent at a show. Give the judge an old-fashioned look if you feel like it, but don't spoil your dog's chances of doing a good scent next time.

A dog's nose, it should be noted, is physically extremely delicate, composed of a series of absorbent, fish-like bones, easily damaged by a blow, readily pained and numbed by a knock, so it is worth remembering that a sharp smack on the nose, so often recommended as the cure for all dog misdemeanours, can result in a run of scent failures for the competitive dog!

Other causes of scent failure can be purely physical, too, such as a cold in the head, failure of the salivary ducts, after effects of anaesthetic (these can last anything up to twelve weeks), and also, of course, the chemical reaction in the body of a bitch immediately before, during and after a season, and the reactions in both dogs and bitches that get the scent of this.

The most common cause, however, for scent failures is the inability of the handler to convey to the dog exactly what is required. One has only to watch a dog rooting among the long grass on a summer's day, excitedly following the trail of some wild creature, to know where his main pleasure in life is hidden. What a pity that some unthinking owners destroy this innocent pleasure when trying to teach competitive work. I should perhaps make it clear at this point that I do *not* include sniffing at lampposts or shop doorways as a legitimate pastime of the dog, and would hasten to recommend that this dangerous habit is nipped in the bud. Many diseases are conveyed through the dog's sniffing in germs as well as appetising smells, and one must be careful that town dogs are given ample opportunity of free runs in country surroundings where they may safely indulge in a good clean sniff.

Unless confused by the handler, a dog can get some of his greatest pleasure in competitive work from the nosework section, which is only a continuation of doing the job he knows best, using the scenting organ that dominates his life. If given the praise and admiration which, after all, a mere human should give to his superior in this field, he thoroughly enjoys showing off his skill.

Before we go into the ways and means of success in competitive nosework, let me make one point perfectly clear. You cannot teach a dog scent. He knows about it already, and you know nothing. All you know is that you or someone else has held a cloth in the hand and you want the dog to pick that particular cloth from a dozen others. Hold a cloth in your hand and then ask a friend to place it among several other similar pieces out of your sight. Now try and pick out the cloth you held. If you can, you are either a superhuman or more likely a bit of a leg puller – you no doubt marked the cloth with a biro before you gave it to your friend! You will see now how outrageous it is when human beings talk about 'teaching' a dog scent. An appropriate parallel would be for a toddler to 'teach' Einstein about relativity.

What we must do, therefore, is (1) have confidence in our dog's nose, and (2) convey to him exactly what is required in competitive nosework. The easiest way to do this is through the Class A scent, which is the handler's scent on the handler's own article to be placed among a number of articles provided by the judge.

Don't start 'teaching' scent, as so many people do, by setting out a number of articles, including their own hotly-scented article, and sending out the dog hopefully. The chances are that every single item in your possession has your scent on it and therefore you are sending the dog out to find your scent among your scent. Not very clever. If by any chance your dog hits the 'correct' article and brings it in, you have not 'taught' him scent, you have done a very stupid thing. You have taught him to bring in the hottest scent he can find from among a lot of cold-scented articles. What usually happens however is for the dog to mouth every single item because they all have your scent on them and he has been sent out to find your scent. You then get annoyed, the dog gets confused and wonders what on earth you want, and all you have done is undermine his confidence in himself and in you, and at the same time have taught him to go out and mouth all sorts of articles.

How, then, are you going to get over to the dog what you want? Over the years I have evolved an extremely satisfactory way of doing this, and I will explain in easy stages. The first thing is that we cannot explain to the dog at this stage what we want, therefore we must get what we want without the possibility of the dog making the slightest mistake. We want him to go out, sniff all the articles until he comes to the right one, pick that up and bring it in, ignoring all the other articles. We do not want him to stand out there looking confused.

This, then, is the method I use to 'teach' scent. During the course of play I find some small article the dog likes and can pick up and hold easily. If I can't find one I make one. A small length of hardboard tubing wrapped in cloth and tied securely with string is excellent. It is easily picked up (the string keeps it just that fraction off the ground and many dogs, particularly flat faced breeds or those without a good scissor bite, find difficulty in picking up articles flush with the ground). We play with the article just for a few seconds each day until he is keyed up for the chance to pick it up. I then sometimes scuff it along the ground or hide it in a place where it is easy for the dog to find. This is aimed at exciting the dog when he recognises 'his' article. You can do all this with a very young puppy once it will pick up an article, but never let him have it more than a couple of times a day or you will defeat the whole object of arousing his interest whenever he sees the article.

I never proceed to the next stage in scent until I have got a good retrieve on a dumb-bell. We are past the play stage now, and embarking on competitive training. Remember I want a good quick scent with no mouthing. Playing tends to encourage mouthing and we must beware of this. On the other hand, the dog's interest and keenness must be maintained. For this reason, you never do scent in the training stages more than twice a day, and when you have trained you never do a successful scent more than once.

I personally never do Class A and B scent after I have got the dog through these classes and into C. There are many Obedience Champions who regularly have to do Class A scents, but I personally have never seen the point of persisting with an exercise once the dog is no longer eligible to go in for it. The only exception I make to this rule is with the Novice Recall which forms part of so many more advanced exercises, including Class C scent.

By all means if your dog enjoys using his nose use your old Class A scent article to give pleasure to him. Throw it in the long grass. Hide it in a chair and let him find it, but don't insist on the present. So long as he does not mouth it or drop it but brings it straight back to you, praise him and let it go at that. If he mouths or starts playing about, forget all about the whole thing. He is obviously getting too excited and thus into bad habits.

Back to our young dog. The next stage (after we have got a retrieve on a dumb-bell) is to do retrieves with the scent article. Make the dog wait while you throw the article, then give him scent lightly placing your hand over the dog's nose. Open your fingers wide. Don't clamp your closed hand over the dog's nose. You will frighten him and cut off his oxygen and then he won't be able to smell anything. Tell the dog to 'Find', and send him off for the article. With luck, he will do a beautiful retrieve and you are on your way to successful scenting.

Figure 6

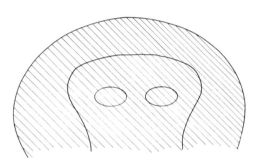

(*a*) A poor way of giving scent. Here the handler smothers the dog's nostrils with hand scent and restricts the passage of air

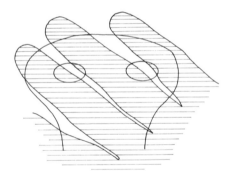

(*b*) A much more satisfactory method. By opening the fingers the handler ensures a free passage of air to the dog's nostrils which enables him to breathe in the scent comfortably

You will note that, up to this stage, I have not mentioned about any other articles being put down, and yet I am saying that you are well on the way to successful scenting. What I am doing is gradually building up in the dog's mind an association between the word 'Find', my hand over his nose, and fetching in an article with my scent on it.

The next stage is to introduce other articles. You remember I explained how important it is never to let the dog mistake our requirements in scent.

We must, therefore, be extremely careful what other articles we put down. We must make sure that they do not hold our scent and that the dog *cannot pick them up even if he wanted to*. As I explained before it is very difficult to find anything in the house that does not carry the occupant's scent. However, certain materials are poor scent carriers, and certain objects are handled little by us. Glass is one such object, and empty milk bottles washed in hot soapy water are ideal if you are extremely careful. Obviously one cannot use this type of article if the dog is a mad, scatty creature likely to try to play football with them, or if he is an exceptionally hard-mouthed and hot-headed fool who will cheerfully damage himself for the sake of a good chew. There is always a danger with glass, and the K.C. has quite rightly banned its use in competitive work. Plastic milk bottles or squash bottles are almost as good for this job and a great deal safer. Metal is another excellent and safe material to use and unopened tins of baked beans make fine 'other' objects. After all, few dogs in their right minds will attempt to pick up a milk bottle or a heavy metal object when their own familiar article is there to be seen.

I start with one other article behind the correct one, building up gradually to eight or nine articles. One way to stimulate keenness if you have somehow blunted it is to let your dog see you throw your own article into the collection. However, it is unlikely, if you have used my method from the start, that the keenness will have gone. You have never let the dog make a mistake and therefore his confidence is intact, also you never do the exercise more than twice a day.

The next stage is to take your dog to training class where there are unfamiliar objects with no danger of your scent being on them. Select (without actually handling) two or three suitably heavy ones and ask someone to be kind enough to put those down for you. Then do your scent. Eureka! A first rate Class A scent in public!

However, things obviously don't always go by the copybook. One of the ways in which you can help your dog is by making absolutely certain that once he has decided which is the correct article and picks it up, he brings it straight out to you. Get him away from the other articles quickly or the temptation may be too much for him and he may put his own article down to investigate something that looks a little more exciting. If necessary, turn round and run away. Do anything to encourage him out of the scent area once he has the correct article in his mouth. The worst thing you can do is to let your dog select his own article and then go on scenting perhaps with his own article still in his mouth, or even dropping it in favour of something else. If you are having difficulty with this, go right back to stage 1, retrieving the article, and then stage 2, using one heavy 'other' article that he cannot pick up and the correct article. If he brings in the wrong article, take it away from him gently, without comment, and go back again to the beginning. Don't shout at him as he is bringing it in or he will hesitate to come to you next time even if he selects the right one. If the dog acts particularly dim-witted you will have to take him up to the correct article and show him. Patience and perseverance now on your part in these early stages will affect your dog's whole scenting career.

When your dog is in competitive Class A then is the time to start 'teaching' Class B scent. This is your scent on the judge's article, several similar articles to be placed in the ring. You will have to be even more careful with your preparation of Class B scent than you were with Class A scent, for by now the dog knows what you want in scent and is not merely retrieving.

The only way to make certain the scent articles do not carry your own scent is to open a new packet of a dozen or so boxes of matches or something similar or get a friend to make up a parcel of empty cigarette packets. Open them without handling, i.e. with scissors or tongs. Hold one for the scent and put the others down in line with the tongs. Don't handle these other objects at all. Show the dog the packet with your scent on so he knows the shape of what he is looking for. Let him do a retrieve on it. Mark it with biro so you will know it again. Then, whilst he is watching, throw it among the other identical packets. Give him scent, then send him to 'find' it. This is the moment of truth for you. Have you taught him to understand what it is you mean by scent? If your dog scents this time you can congratulate yourself on getting over to him what you want. He will have to scent this time even though he has seen it thrown in and knows it is there somewhere. It is unlikely he will have marked the exact spot. Remember you have thrown it. It has not been placed, a much slower and more deliberate process, and therefore much easier for the dog to mark.

The next stages are to attempt the scent without letting the dog have the object first, then to have the object placed for you with the dog turned away, and then with a hot decoy in it.

It is a fact that never fails to astonish some competitors that when a dog starts Class C scent he never fails. Until one day he does, and from that time on he is never reliable. The answer is simple. The dog has never been given the benefit of sharing with his handler the knowledge of what is required in scent. If he had he would not make these mistakes. The dog that has been successfully brought up through Class A and Class B scent as explained so far is excellent material for successful Class C scent.

The dog is not now required to pick out your scent. He is required to pick out a stranger's scent on cloth, several similar pieces of cloth, some or all of them decoyed, to be around the ring. The first thing to make sure of is that your dog will pick up cloth. Find a piece and back we go to Stage 1 with our retrieve.

Having ensured there is no difficulty here, we are now ready to try a stranger's scent. We must not do this until we have one or two things clear in our own minds. In the first place, remember this is *not* your scent, it is someone else's. The dog, therefore, must know before we send him out that here is something different. It is no use saying to him 'Find'. That to the dog means find your handler's scent. But the handler's scent is not there. The command now must be 'Seek' – to differentiate between 'Find my scent' and 'Seek his scent'.

It is very important in the early stages of Class C to do scent on a 'familiar' stranger. Double Dutch, no doubt, but you know what I mean. I always use my husband, and I advise always using someone the dog knows and likes.

Now, difficult though it has been to get Class A and Class B articles without your scent, it is well nigh impossible to prepare cloths without your scent. The best method is to get someone else who is interested in Class C scent to prepare your cloths from his own material and you return the compliment by preparing some for him. The best scent holders are torn up old sheets and pillow cases. Make as many 7 in. × 7 in. squares as you can. Fold them neatly into a big, airtight glass jar or heavy-duty polythene bag tied securely at the top with elastic bands. When you receive your bundle, get them out of your car as soon as you can, and don't bring them into your house. Place the container in an outhouse or garage. In this way you can be almost certain that there will be little if any of your scent or that of any of the other members of your household on the cloths. Don't handle these cloths at any time. Remember you are asking the dog to find someone else's scent. Your scent is strongest in his mind, and it is confusing to a dog seeking someone else's scent to come across yours. For this reason, never act as decoy for your own dog. The dog has been taught for too long to recognise your scent to lightly discard it and at best you will confuse him and take his attention away from the job in hand. At worst you will undo all the hard work you have put into teaching your dog what you mean by 'scent'.

When the time comes to do scent, it is best to have the help of two people, one to act as the judge and take two cloths from the jar, one to act as steward and put down the cloths for you. Don't do complicated patterns when you are in the early stages with a dog. Make it as simple as possible. A straight line due north from the dog is by far the easiest for him to follow. Put two or three blanks (in actual fact these will carry the scent of the friend who prepared them for you plus the scent of whoever puts them down, so they are really lightly-scented decoys) and one lightly-scented cloth from the judge down, and then take the second lightly-scented cloth from him. Place it carefully over the dog's nose forming an air pocket underneath. If the dog is worried, loosen the cloth immediately. If he is unworried, try and get him to hold it as well as have it over his nose. Quickly give him the command 'Seek', helped with a hand signal indicating the cloths, and let him go. If he hesitates over the correct cloth, call his name pleasantly and get him in with the cloth. Don't say 'Hold' or 'Seek' at this point. His attention may be on the wrong cloth by the time you have got the word out, and the last thing you want is confusion or the wrong cloth. His name called pleasantly will make him look up and the chances are his decision will be made for him. He will pick up the correct cloth and come in to you.

If you do not succeed, reduce the cloths, even to the point of only having the correct cloth down, so that he has no choice but to bring in the right one. As soon as you have got him going out and bringing in the correct one from a choice of four, start putting in 'light' decoys, anyone's scent except your own and of course the judge's. It is good practice to use a lot of decoys, but don't forget your blanks as well. They are very important.

At no time alter the 'judge'. It must always be the same person. Always. Many dogs are ruined in Class C scent through having first one scent to find, then another, then another. In practice, never use anyone except your original choice. In the ring, of course, you will do the judge of the day's scent, but never do a true stranger's scent more than once a week. When in competition my dogs do a scent once a week – in the Championship show ring! Occasionally they will have a practice at class on my husband's scent, but usually only if I haven't a show lined up for them that week. Many people prefer to do only Class B scents on cloth (that is their own scent rather than someone else's) never practising Class C at all. If this works well with their dogs, it would be foolish to change.

Whatever you do, never reprimand a dog over scent. If he fails at a show, grin and bear it. You cannot possibly know what the judge has been up to with his cloths, so treat the whole thing as 'one of those things'. Have a practice at home or at class in a day or so, but go back to your familiar 'judge', and when the dog brings the right one out remember to give lavish praise. If the dog fails at class or at home, suspect your own carelessness first, after that reduce the number of cloths drastically until you can build up again to a dozen.

I think it is important to indicate to the dog that you are not particularly happy about him bringing in a decoy or a blank, and I have never been able to follow the reasoning behind some handlers going into ecstasy when their dog brings in the decoy. However, you must indicate in a way that will not discourage him from trying again another time. I step forward and gently take the cloth from my dog rather than let him present it. This is quite sufficient 'correction'.

If you have read this far I am quite sure that you will not be the type of person to shout or wave your arms around in a fury or do anything similar to scare your dog off the cloths, but I'm afraid many handlers who should know better do when a 'ticket' has just gone down the drain through scent failure, and then they wonder why their dogs are never reliable in scent. They forget that what you do today will affect next week's show. If you do let rip because you have lost a ticket today, the chances are that next time you are in the lead and the pressure is on, the dog will sense the tension, become apprehensive and in sheer desperation he will either refuse to pick up the correct cloth even though he knows it is the right one, or else he will panic and pick up anything. His concentration will be shattered and it will take anything up to twelve months to get his confidence back again. Remember, please, he *knows* about scent, we don't.

Faults such as playing about, or chewing, must be corrected at the retrieve stage, and if they develop later on you must go right back. If you are having difficulty with the present you must go right back to Novice recalls. Remember Golden Rule No. 7: *Break Up the Exercise and Build It up in Easy Steps.* Never spoil the important part of the exercise, e.g. the actual scenting, because of minor details in present or mouthing.

9 More about Nosework

Searching: Tracking: Gunshot: Speaking on Command

The Working Trials Companion Dog Stake search is done in an area 15 yards square. Other Stakes are in areas 25 yards square. Most search articles (which are always provided by the judge) are considerably smaller than anything that is used in the Obedience ring, and it is a good idea to encourage your dog to pick out a variety of small things, match boxes, *blunted* 6-in. nails, tops of the cheap type of ball point pens, etc. from coarse grass. Don't go mad. Don't throw articles miles away. Drop them quite close to the dog but encourage him to use his nose and actually search.

If you do not intend to combine competitive Obedience work with Trials work you shouldn't have too many problems, but you will ruin a dog for Obedience scenting if you are not clever enough to make it absolutely clear in the dog's mind the difference between scenting and searching. Use a completely different command, 'Where is it then?' for searching out strange articles in Trials, and remember that to a trained Obedience dog you are now asking him to bring out hot decoys, something you have been trying to teach him NOT to do in Obedience! The Trials dog is expected to pick out these hot articles without the benefit of matching up scent with the judge – a very, very dodgy occupation until you have those precious three Obedience Certificates safely tucked under your belt!

Once the dog has got the idea of searching through grass to find the article, move on to the area you have selected for your search area practice. Mark it with broom handles or poles of some kind. You can't possibly guess 15 yards square and you must have an accurate idea of how big the area is. I know, it looks enormous!

The first thing to do is to decide which way the wind is blowing. This is important because if you have the wind behind you blowing past you on to the area, your scent will carry over the area and possibly mask the scent from the article. In addition, the scent from the article will blow away from the dog and instead of meeting the scent *before* he actually gets to the article he will in fact have to go *past* the article and come back. As you are timed in this exercise, precious moments might be lost, and also you are making the dog work in adverse conditions.

Move around the outside of the area until you get the wind blowing straight at you. One excellent way of finding out how the wind is blowing is to pluck a handful of grass and throw it in the air. If it comes back in your face you are in the ideal position. I remember one very well-known Trials personality who always does this little trick doubling up with laughter when she overheard two raw novices deep in conversation. 'Why do you do that?' asked A as B plucked some grass and threw it in the air. 'I don't know really,' confessed B, 'but Mrs X always does it.' I suppose she thought it was some ritualistic ceremony that had to be performed before you were allowed to compete! Anyway what was good enough for the successful Mrs X was good enough for her, even if she hadn't a clue what it was all about!

The next step is to let your dog see you throw your article or, better still, two or three articles into the centre of the square. Give your command. In Trials you must learn to 'read' your dog a great deal more than is called for in Obedience work, and you will have to recognise his reactions when he is near the scent. Give encouragement to 'Find' in an excited tone of voice if he indicates that he is near the article. Do nothing to distract his attention from the job in hand, and if his attention wanders get him back on the job as quickly as you can. Make it easy going at first. Although in competition you may not go inside the area, you can move around the outside, giving as many commands as you want. In practice, however, I believe in going inside the area with an inexperienced dog until he has sufficient confidence to work the area on his own. It is a poor reflection on some type of Obedience training that many Obedience trained dogs will not work on their own initiative but have to be coaxed into thinking for themselves. In Trials work it is essential for the dog to think things out for himself and not rely on his handler to tell him everything. Sadly, some methods of training Obedience dogs takes away much of this initiative.

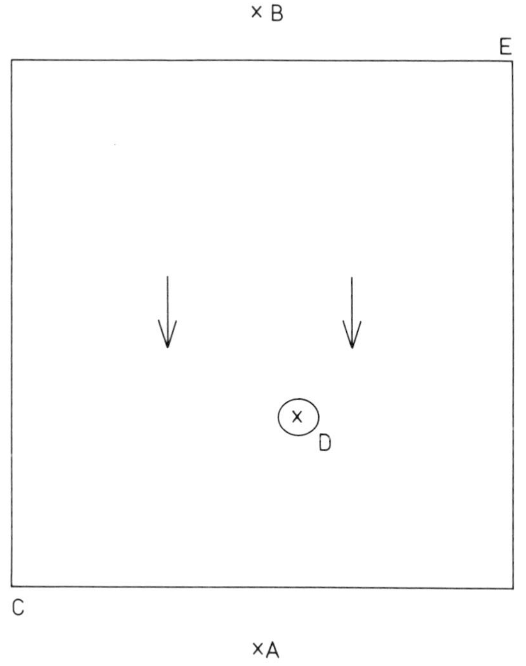

Figure 7. Wind direction in the Search. Handler A stands in the correct position with the wind blowing directly at him. He is helping his dog to wind scent the article D. The dog will enter the area from point C and the scent from the article will reach him before he actually gets to the article itself. The handler's scent is blowing away from the area and thus not hindering the dog's search. Handler B is making things very difficult for his dog who will enter at point E. The handler's scent is fouling the area and the dog will have to go right up to the article or even beyond it before he strikes the scent which is being blown away from him

If, as sometimes happens, neither your dog nor you can find the article, quickly drop something quite close to the dog, encourage him to find it and get him out with lavish praise. Your dog must always be successful in searching and in tracking. His interest will very quickly evaporate if he has a few disappointments. The great difference between Obedience and Working Trials is that in Obedience a skilful handler can often take a mediocre dog to the top. In Working Trials it is the talented dog that frequently takes the mediocre handler to the top. There is so much in Working Trials where the dog must work on his own initiative that the most important part the handler can play is in morale boosting.

You will have to get your dog used to quartering the ground. Lucky the handler who has a spaniel on this job, for quartering is a built-in instinct with that breed. However, most working dogs can give a good acount of themselves in quartering if given the correct initial training and encouragement. Some judges are nasty enough to drop the articles on the actual outside line of the area, so get your dog to start up-wind from about 18 in. in front of the front line. Encourage him to work the line A–B shown in the illustration before allowing him to move up a yard to C. Encourage him to work C–D before moving up to E. Then comes E–F. Move on to G and work G–H, and so on. This is the ideal, and few dogs in the excitement of test conditions will do this, but try for perfection of style at least in practice. Get him to recognise those poles and to know that somewhere in between lies his goal.

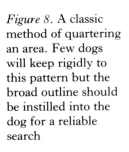

Figure 8. A classic method of quartering an area. Few dogs will keep rigidly to this pattern but the broad outline should be instilled into the dog for a reliable search

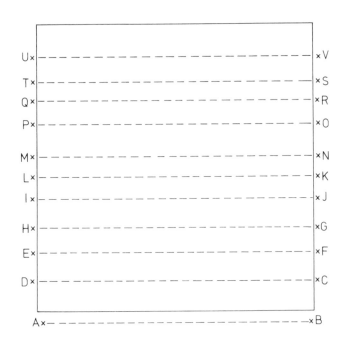

Tracking

Although you may have to do your track on the same day as your Search in actual competition, in practice, and certainly in the early stages, don't do track and search on the same day. You will need a 12-yard minimum length of tracking line and a good quality harness that is comfortable for the dog to wear. It is a good plan to get the dog used to his harness and line before teaching tracking and then, each time you practise, go through the rigmarole of putting on his harness and line. This indicates to the dog exactly what the exercise is. Never use his harness at any time other than when he is to track.

Begin with a short track of three or four yards. Scuff your feet along the grass so that you actually dent the grass and snap off some of the longer tips. With the dog watching, place a conspicuous object, such as a well-scented cloth on the end of your track, and then return along the same route, shuffling your feet as you come. Hold the dog on a short line (if you can't cope with 12 yards at this stage, use two leads clipped together), encourage him to put his nose on the start of the track and tell him to 'Track'. If he keeps his nose down you are doing well. The chances are, however, that he will make straight for the cloth, which of course he can see. Don't give any pull on the line. Let him get to the object his way and let him pick it up and present it. Give him lavish praise.

Next, put a smaller item down that he can't see, and again encourage him to put his nose down at the start of the track, and this time he may well follow the track successfully and get to the article. Encourage him to pick it up and present. Give lavish praise again. Gradually, as the days go by increase the length of the track, always putting one article about three or four yards away and lengthening the distance to the second article. Do remember where you have put the track! It's the easiest thing in the world to forget, and then your work is useless for that day!

Keep behind your dog, otherwise you will foul the track, and let the *dog* do the tracking. Don't think that because you know where the article is you should haul him along on his line to it. He must find out his own method of tracking. If he is a persistent type of dog who seldom raises his nose from the scent until he has reached the article, you are very lucky and will probably do well with him. If, however, he is a wind scenter, don't try to teach him to keep his nose on the track. He won't do it and, you will spoil his natural ability. Don't let this type of dog get too far away from the track in practice, or he will quickly lose the scent when it comes to competition work and there are plenty of bends and angles along the track.

In search and track it is essential to praise the attempt. Build up the dog's confidence in his own achievements. Make it all quite easy to start with. A dog will quickly become depressed on the track, so make sure you keep the lessons short and pleasant. He must always be successful, and if you and he lose the track and the articles along it, get him back to where you know the track is, even if it means going almost back to the start, and drop an article on it a few yards ahead of him. Encourage him on and let him find the article, so that once again he is successful.

A dog will quickly get physically tired through the effort of tracking and using his nose with so much concentration. Once the dog is trained, never do a track more than once a week. Although the time allowed for a track is stipulated in the rules, you won't worry about this until a much later stage. Tracks laid by a stranger are up to three hours old in the senior stakes, but for heaven's sake, do your own tracks and send the dog off on them immediately in the early stages.

Gradually build up to the stage where you can ask a friend to mark a track for you and increase the length of time it has been down.

It is a good idea to plant one of your broomsticks at the start of your track, with a second one several yards ahead. This indicates to the dog where the start of the track is and gives him confidence that he is, literally, 'on the right track'.

Although there are a hundred-and-one distractions on the average track (cross-tracks, animal scents, etc.) a good, keen tracking dog will persevere with his original scent. It is up to the handler to see that his keenness and ability are always encouraged.

Steadiness to gunshot

To get a dog steady to gunshot, do it gradually and don't make a lot of fuss over it. Have a friend fire a small calibre pistol or a child's cap pistol a long way off while you are doing a spot of Heelwork with your dog. If he barks at the noise take little notice, except to reassure him that all is well. However, whatever you do, don't make a 'thing' out of it and thus instil in the dog the idea that this is something terrible to happen. Few dogs will rush off if a gun is fired initially at a distance, although many will be thoroughly frightened if introduced to gunshot close by. When you are sure he is not bothered at distant firing, bring your friend nearer for the next report. Repeat as above. If the dog is unworried close the gap between the shot and the dog, until he will tolerate quite close firing.

One safety note: I expect you are aware that under no circumstances whatsoever should your friend point the pistol at either you or your dog. Apart from the danger of burns or shock, almost invariably a threat of this nature will incite the dog to attack.

Speaking on command

It is much easier to teach a dog to speak on command than it is to shut him up once he has grown to like the idea! When the dog is barking at something, perhaps someone knocking at the door, encourage him by telling him how clever he is and repeating the word 'Speak, speak. Good boy, speak'. When he has grasped what you want, then say, 'Quiet' and insist on just that. If necessary, take hold of the dog by the collar and put your hand over his mouth to keep it shut. When he is quiet, praise him and leave it for the time being. Next opportunity go through the routine again until you have got him barking because he likes it, but immediately responsive to the command to stop. Next try him without the outside stimulus of door knocking, and see if you can get him going. This may take some time for him to realise you want him speaking without a cause, but once he is speaking and knows you are pleased, insist that he quietens on command.

Police Dog

Teaching a dog Police Dog work is outside the scope of this book. In fact, apart from policemen and the most knowledgeable of handlers, it should really be outside the requirements of most dog owners. It is an unfortunate fact that a badly-trained or even a partly-trained P.D. dog is a menace. Many so-called 'guard-dogs' have a modicum of P.D. training and are almost completely unmanageable in many instances. A true Police-trained dog is one of the wonders of the canine world, but the job must be done properly. Few civilians, apart from a few highly-skilled handlers of Working Trial dogs, can hope to achieve the same degree of perfection in training that is demanded by the Police, and, when one considers what a weapon an attacking dog can be, one appreciates that it should be left to the Police and the highly responsible few to train for this work. A dog that has been trained to attack, for instance, can mistake an innocent person running for a bus as a fleeing criminal unless he has been taught otherwise, and a dog that cannot be called off attack is a potential killer. You will appreciate, therefore, why I have no intention of covering this type of training in a book for public consumption. You can make up your Working Trials Champion, if that is your ultimate ambition, on tracking alone without any need for P.D. work.

10 Summing up

Now that you have trained your dog, what are the pitfalls? One thing you will have to watch out for is boredom. The canine mind quickly becomes bored with the sameness of routine training and there is no point in practising something that the dog does perfectly. A once-weekly run through is plenty for the dog that makes no mistakes. Someone once asked me how much time I spent training Fern the year she hit her peak. My reply shattered him. I told him she never saw a scent cloth, never did Heelwork, Sendaway, Retrieve, Distant Control, from one show to the next. She did do a five minute Sit every single day, though, to remind her that I wasn't very keen on losing ten points on such an elementary exercise. With another dog, it may be necessary to train three times a day every day of the week to constantly remind him of what he is expected to do. The secret lies in knowing your dog. Few dogs will accept a huge amount of training cheerfully, however, and I feel it better to sacrifice a little accuracy at times for the sake of enthusiasm, rather than to have a technically perfect round devoid of zip.

Keep on training new exercises with your dog. Communication is the great thing, and so long as you and your dog are working happily together it does not really matter what you are doing. Win or not, if you and your dog enjoy each other's company and you enjoy training together, you will reap plenty of rewards in and out the ring.

I hope I have not given the impression in this book that the methods of training advocated herein are the only means. People achieve success in different ways. For them, their ways are obviously the best. I could not cope with some methods, particularly the more complicated ones, and I have found by trial, error and eventual success that the methods which suit me best are basically simple. Thus I have written them down in the hope that they may be of use to others. Perhaps mine are not the best methods for your dog. If not, you must search around until you find something more suitable. I hope, however, that somewhere in these pages you will have found something of practical use to shine a light in a darkened corner.

As one who enjoys actively partaking in competition by penning my thoughts and training ideas in the form of a book, perhaps I am inviting some unkind remarks from fellow competitors who disagree with my methods. I hope, however, that the majority of readers will accept this book in the manner that it was written – as a practical guide to aspiring obedience handlers, competitors or not, and to all, in fact, who seek to understand dogs better and, by greater understanding, achieve a fuller partnership.

Whatever method you choose, however, I hope you will bear in mind my paraphrase of the immortal Bard who always expressed things so much better than anyone else: 'The fault, dear trainers, lies not in our stars nor in our dogs, but in ourselves'.

In summing up I would strongly advise you to try and train with and compete against others considerably better than yourself. This way you will improve. To always be the best in the class or in the show is the road to complacency. A thought which should sober you is that when you reach the top, there is only one way to go – downwards!

And finally, don't trust to luck. Of course luck does come into winning prizes, but why rely on good luck to get you to the top and blame bad luck for your failures? Train your dog to as near perfection as you can get. Know when you go in the ring that he is capable of doing every exercise and every part of every exercise perfectly because that is the way he has been trained. Then bad luck, and bad luck alone can defeat you. On the day that Lady Luck smiles, you will be unbeatable.

A recap on the Golden Rules of Dog Training:
1 Prevention is better than cure.
2 Each dog is an individual. Know your dog.
3 Be consistent.
4 In practice, always praise the attempt.
5 Correction and praise are the basis of all training.
6 Make absolutely certain in your own mind what you want from the dog before you start to train.
7 Break up each exercise into small sections and then fit it together like a jigsaw. Don't destroy the part that is good in an effort to correct the weakest part.
8 Dogs have off days the same as we do. They are not machines. Never train if you are tired or fed up or if the dog is.
9 Make sure the dog understands when he is working and when he is free.
10 Timing is the key to successful training.
11 Patience and perseverance are the hallmark of a good trainer.
12 Get your dog's attention and keep it.

Appendix 1

Kennel Club regulations for Tests for Obedience Classes

Reproduced by kind permission of the Kennel Club

A Show Society may schedule any or all of the following classes at a show. No variation to any test within a class may be made. 'Run-offs' will be judged, one at a time, by normal scheduled tests.

Classes may be placed in any order in the schedule but this order must be followed at the show except that a Society, by publication in the schedule, may reserve the right to vary the order of judging when the entry is known.

The maximum number of entries permitted in a Class for one Judge to judge with the exception of Class C where Obedience Certificates are on offer shall be sixty. If this number is exceeded the Class shall be divided by a draw into two equal halves, each to be judged separately. The prizes for each Class shall be the same as that offered for the original Class. No Judge shall judge more than sixty dogs in one day and if a Judge is appointed for two or more Classes the combined total entries of which exceed sixty, a Reserve Judge shall be called upon to officiate appropriately. Show Societies should ensure that when appointing Judges for Shows sufficient numbers are appointed for the expected entries. The Reserve Judge may enter dogs for competition at the Show and if not called upon to judge may compete.

Where a Class is divided into two halves exhibitors who have entered for that Class shall be notified accordingly of all changes or alterations and no timed stay exercises are to be held earlier than those advertised for the original class.

In Class C where Obedience Certificates are on offer one Judge only may be appointed for each sex. Judges must be present at all times dogs are under test including stay exercises.

In all the classes the handler may use the dog's name with a command or signal without penalty. Except in the Stay Tests, and Distant Control, all tests shall commence and finish with the dog sitting at the handler's side except in Beginners, Novice and Class A Recall Tests when the dog may be left in either the Sit or Down position at the handler's choice.

Food shall not be given to a dog in the ring.

In any test in which judge's articles are used, none of them should be injurious to the dog, and they must be capable of being picked up by any breed entered in that test.

Spayed bitches and castrated dogs are permitted to compete in Obedience Classes.

No bitch in season shall be allowed to compete in Obedience Classes.

In all tests the points must be graduated.

Handlers may use only a slip chain or smooth collar in the ring.

Every handler must wear his ring number prominently displayed when in the ring.

The Show Executive shall appoint a Chief Steward, whose name must be announced in the schedule and who must not work a dog at the Show. The Chief Steward shall be responsible for the control of any running order and for the smooth running of each class, and whose decision in such matters shall be final.

A draw for the order of running in Class C at a Championship Show must be made prior to the Show and exhibitiors and judges must be notified of the order of running before the day of the show. The Kennel Club will ballot for the running order for Championship Class C and Show Secretaries must forward lists of entries by recorded delivery or registered post to the Kennel Club for a ballot within 7 days after the closing of entries. Where a complete draw for the running order of classes other than Championship Class C is not made, Show Managements must ensure that at least 10 competitors/dogs are available by means of a ballot for judging in the first hour following the scheduled time for the commencement of judging of that class and these competitors must be notified prior to the Show. All competitors must report to the Ring Scoreboard Steward and book in within one hour of the scheduled time for the commencement of judging for the class and those reporting late will be excluded from competition unless they have reported previously to the Chief Steward that they are actually working a dog entered in another Championship Class C or in the Stay Tests of another class. Where a complete running order is made, all competitors must be notified prior to the day of the Show and must book in on arrival at the Show. Published orders of running must be strictly adhered to.

Where timed stays will take place it must be announced in the schedule that they take priority over other tests, the times of such tests to be promulgated at the Show and published in the catalogue. In the case of Championship Class C stays must not be judged before 1 p.m.

Where Championship Class C competitors are required to compete in another Class at the Show the Chief Steward will agree with the judges of these other classes that the judging of such competitors be re-arranged in the running order. It will be the responsibility of competitors to advise the Chief Steward of the clash of judging.

In all Scent Tests, dogs should compete in the same order as for previous tests, but the judge may relax the running order where necessary. Scent tests must not be carried out during the main ring work but will take place as a separate test at the judges' discretion.

Judging rings shall not in any circumstances contain less than 900 square feet of clear floor space and shall be not less than 20 feet in width except that for Championship Class C the ring must contain not less than 1,600 square feet.

No person shall carry out punitive correction or harsh handling of a dog at any time whilst within the boundaries of the show.

Imperfections in heeling between tests will not be judged but any physical disciplining by the handler in the ring, or any uncontrolled behaviour of the dog, such as snapping, unjustified barking, fouling the ring, or running out of the ring, even between tests, must be penalised by deducting points from the total score and the judge may bar the dog from further competition in that class.

In all the following Definitions of Classes, First Prize wins in Limited and Sanction Show Obedience Classes will not count for entry in Open and Championship Show Obedience Classes. No dog is eligible to compete in Obedience Classes at Limited and Sanction Shows which has won an Obedience Certificate or obtained any award that counts towards the title of Obedience Champion or the equivalent thereof under the rules of any governing body recognised by the Kennel Club. Obedience Champions are eligible only for Class C at Open and Championship Shows.

A dog may be entered in any two classes at a Show for which it is eligible with the exception of Championship Class C for which only dogs appropriately qualified may be entered. (Note the qualification for Championship Class C and Obedience Warrant.)

PRE-BEGINNERS – Pre-Beginners Classes may only be scheduled at Limited and Sanction Obedience Shows. If owner or handler or dog have won a first prize in any Class they may not compete in Pre-Beginners.

Handlers will not be penalised for encouragement or extra commands except in the Sit and Down tests. In these tests, at the discretion of the judge, handlers may face their dogs. Judges or Stewards must not use the words 'last command' except in the Sit and Down tests.

1 Heel on Lead — 15 points
2 Heel Free — 20 points
3 Recall from sit or down position at handler's choice. Dog to be recalled by handler when stationary and facing the dog. Dog to return smartly to the handler, sit in front, go to heel—all on command of judge or steward to handler. Distance at discretion of judge. Test commences when handler leaves dog — 10 points

4	Sit One Minute, handler in sight	10 points
5	Down Two Minutes, handler in sight	20 points
		TOTAL 75 points

BEGINNERS – If owner or handler or dog have won a total of two or more first prizes in the Beginners Class, they may not compete in Beginners. Winners of one first prize in any other Obedience Class are ineligible to compete in this Class.

Handlers will not be penalised for encouragement or extra commands except in the Sit and Down tests. In these tests, at the discretion of the judge, handlers may face their dogs. Judges or stewards must not use the words 'last command' except in the Sit and Down tests.

1 Heel on Lead — 15 points
2 Heel Free — 20 points
3 Recall from sit or down position at handler's choice. Dog to be recalled by handler when stationary and facing the dog. Dog to return smartly to handler, sit in front, go to heel – all on command of judge or steward to handler. Distance at discretion of judge. Test commences when handler leaves dog. — 10 points
4 Retrieve any article. Handlers may use their own article. — 25 points
5 Sit One Minute, handler in sight. — 10 points
6 Down Two Minutes, handler in sight — 20 points

TOTAL 100 points

NOVICE – For dogs that have not won two first prizes in Obedience Classes (Beginners Class excepted).

Handlers will not be penalised for encouragement or extra commands except in the Sit and Down tests. In these tests, at the discretion of the judge, handlers may face their dogs. Judges or stewards must not use the words 'last command' except in the Sit and Down tests.

1 Temperament Test. To take place immediately before heel on lead. Dog to be on lead in the Stand position. Handler to stand by dog. Judge to approach quietly from the front and to run his hand gently down the dog's back. Judge may talk quietly to dog to reassure it. Any undue resentment, cringing, growling or snapping to be penalised. This is not a stand for examination or stay test. — 10 points
2 Heel on Lead — 10 points
3 Heel Free — 20 points

4 Recall from sit or down position at handler's choice. Dog to be recalled by handler when stationary and facing the dog. Dog to return smartly to handler, sit in front, go to heel – all on command of judge or steward to handler. Distance at discretion of judge. Test commences when handler leaves dog.   10 points

5 Retrieve a Dumb-bell. Handlers may use their own bells   20 points

6 Sit One Minute, handler in sight   10 points

7 Down Two minutes, handler in sight   20 points

TOTAL 100 points

CLASS A – For dogs which have not won three first prizes in Classes A, B and open Class C in total.

Simultaneous command and signal will be permitted. Extra commands or signals must be penalised.

1 Heel on Lead   15 points

2 Temperament Test. Will take place before Heel Free. Dog to be in the stand position and off lead. Handler to stand beside dog. Conditions as for Novice Temperament Test, except that Test will commence with order 'last command' and end with order 'test finished'. Extra commands will be penalised. This is not a stand for examination or stay test.   10 points

3 Heel Free   20 points

4 Recall from Sit or Down, position at handler's choice. Dog to be recalled to heel by handler, on command of judge or steward, whilst handler is walking away from dog, both to continue forward until halted. The recall and halt points to be the same for each dog and handler. Test commences following handler's last command to dog.   15 points

5 Retrieve a Dumb-bell. Handlers may use their own dumb-bells   20 points

6 Sit One Minute, handler in sight   10 points

7 Down Five Minutes, handler out of sight   30 points

8 Scent Discrimination, handler's scent on handler's article. The total number of articles shall not exceed ten, all of which shall be clearly visible to the dog.   30 points

TOTAL 150 points

CLASS B – For dogs which have not won three first prizes in Class B and Open Class C in total.

One command, by word or signal, except in Test 2. Extra commands or signals must be penalised.

1. Heel Free. The dog shall be required to walk at heel free and shall also be tested at fast and slow pace. Each change of pace shall commence from the 'halt' position — 30 points
2. Send Away, Drop and Recall. On command of judge to handler, dog to be sent away in direction indicated by judge. After the dog has been dropped, handler will call the dog to heel whilst walking where directed by judge and both will continue forward. No obstacle to be placed in path of dog. Simultaneous command and signal is permitted but as soon as the dog leaves the handler the arm must be dropped. (N.B. an extra command may be simultaneous command and signal, but an extra command must be penalised) — 40 points
3. Retrieve any one article provided by the Judge but which must not be in any manner injurious to the dog (definitely excluding food or glass). The article to be picked up easily by any breed of dog in that Class and to be clearly visible to the dog. A separate similar article to be used for each dog. Test commences following Judge or Steward's words 'last command' to handler. — 30 points
4. Stand One Minute, handler at least ten paces away from and facing away from the dog — 10 points
5. Sit Two Minutes, handler out of sight — 20 points
6. Down Ten Minutes, handler out of sight — 40 points
7. Scent Discrimination. Handler's scent on article provided by judge. A separate similar article to be used for each dog and the total number of articles shall not exceed ten, all of which shall be clearly visible to the dog and shall be similar to the article given to the handler. Judges must use a separate similar scent decoy or decoy for each dog. No points will be awarded if the article is given to the dog. — 30 points

TOTAL 200 points

CLASS C – At Championship Shows: For dogs which have been placed on at least one occasion not lower than third in each class of Novice Class, Class A and Class B and have won Open Class C with not less than 290 marks on one occasion and have gained at least 290 marks in Open Class C on three further occasions under different judges. Dogs which qualified for entry in Championship Class C prior to 1st May 1980 are also eligible.

At Limited and Sanction Shows: Open to all dogs except

Obedience Certificate winners and dogs which have obtained any award that counts towards the title of Obedience Champion or the equivalent thereof under the rules of any governing body recognised by the Kennel Club.

One command, by word or signal, except in Test 2 where an extra command may be simultaneous command and signal. Extra commands or signals must be penalised.

1 Heel Work. The dog shall be required to walk at heel free, and also be tested at fast and slow pace. At some time during this test, at the discretion of the judge, the dog shall be required, whilst walking to heel at normal pace, to be left at the Stand, Sit and Down in any order (the order to be the same for each dog) as and when directed by the judge. The handler shall continue forward alone, without hesitation, and continue as directed by the judge until he reaches his dog when both shall continue forward together until halted. Heel work may include left about turns and figure-of-eight at normal and/or slow pace   60 points

2 Send Away, Drop and Recall as in Class B   40 points

3 Retrieve any one article provided by the Judge but which must not be in any manner injurious to the dog (definitely excluding food or glass). The article to be picked up easily by any breed of dog in that Class and to be clearly visible to the dog. A separate similar article to be used for each dog. Test commences following Judge or Steward's 'last command' to handler   30 points

4 Distant Control. Dog to Sit, Stand and Down at a marked place not less than ten paces from handler, in any order on command from judge to handler. Six instructions to be given in the same order for each dog. Excessive movement, i.e. more than the length of the dog, in any direction by the dog, having regard to its size, will be penalised. The dog shall start the exercise with its front feet behind a designated point. No penalty for excessive movement in a forward direction shall be imposed until the back legs of the dog pass the designated point.   50 points

5 Sit Two Minutes, handler out of sight   20 points

6 Down Ten Minutes, handler out of sight   50 points

7 Scent Discrimination. Judge's scent on piece of marked cloth. Neutral and decoy cloths to be provided by the Show Executive. The judge shall not place his cloth in the ring himself, but it shall be placed by a steward. A

separate similar piece to be used for each dog and the total number of separate similar pieces of cloth from which the dog shall discriminate shall not exceed ten. If a dog fetches or fouls a wrong article this must be replaced by a fresh article. At open-air shows all scent cloths must be adequately weighted to prevent them being blown about. The method of taking scent shall be at the handler's discretion but shall not require the judge to place his hand on or lean towards the dog. A separate similar piece of cloth approximately 6 in. by 6 in. but not more than 10 in. by 10 in. shall be available to be used for giving each dog the scent. Judges should use a scent decoy or decoys   50 points

TOTAL 300 points

The Kennel Club will offer an Obedience Certificate (Dog) and an Obedience Certificate (Bitch) for winners of 1st prizes in Class C Dog and Class C Bitch at a Championship Show, provided that the exhibits do not lose more than 10 points out of 300, and provided also that the classes are open to all breeds.

Judges must also award a Reserve Best of Sex provided that the exhibit has not lost more than 10 points out of 300.

The Kennel Club will offer at Crufts Dog Show each year the Kennel Club Obedience Championship – (Dog) and the Kennel Club Obedience Championship – (Bitch). A dog awarded one or more Obedience Certificates during the calendar year preceding Crufts Show shall be entitled to compete.

The Tests for the Championships shall be those required for Class C in these Regulations. If the winning dog or bitch has lost more than 10 points out of 300, the Championship award shall be withheld.

As provided in Kennel Club Rule 4(c), the following dogs shall be entitled to be described as Obedience Champions and shall receive a Certificate to that effect from the Kennel Club:—

(a) The winners of the Kennel Club Obedience Championships.
(b) A dog awarded three Obedience Certificates under three different judges in accordance with these Regulations.

Explanatory notes for Obedience Tests

In all classes the dog should work in a happy natural manner and prime consideration should be given to judging the dog and handler as a team. The dog may be encouraged and praised except where specifically stated.

Instructions and commands to competitors may be made either by the judge or his steward by delegation.

In all tests the left side of a handler will be regarded as the 'working side', unless the handler suffers from a physical disability and has the judge's permission to work the dog from the right-hand side.

To signal the completion of each test the handler will be given the command 'test finished'.

It is permissible for handlers to practise their dogs before going into the ring provided there is no punitive correction and this is similar to an athlete limbering up before an event.

The dog should be led into the ring for judging with a collar and lead attached (unless otherwise directed) and should be at the handler's side.

1 Heel on Lead – The dog should be sitting straight at the handler's side. On command the handler should walk briskly forward in a straight line with the dog at heel. The dog should be approximately level with and reasonably close to the handler's leg at all times when the handler is walking. The lead must be slack at all times. On the command 'Left Turn' or 'Right Turn' the handler should turn smartly at a right angle in the appropriate direction and the dog should keep its position at the handler's side. Unless otherwise directed, at the command 'about turn' the handler should turn about smartly on the spot through an angle of 180° to the right and walk in the opposite direction, the dog maintaining its position at the handler's side. On the command 'halt' the handler should halt immediately and the dog should sit straight at the handler's side. Throughout this test the handler may not touch the dog or make use of the lead without penalty.

2 Heel Free – This test should be carried out in a similar manner as for Heel on Lead except that the dog must be off the lead throughout the test.

3 Retrieve a Dumb-Bell/Article – At the start of this exercise the dog should be sitting at the handler's side. On command the handler must throw the dumb-bell/article in the direction indicated. The dog should remain at the Sit position until the handler is ordered to send it to retrieve the dumb-bell/article. The dog should move out promptly at a smart pace to collect the dumb-bell/article cleanly. It should return with the dumb-bell/article at a smart pace and sit straight in front of the handler. On command the handler should take the dumb-bell/article from the dog. On further command the dog should be sent to heel. In Classes A, B and C the test commences on the order 'last command' to handler.

4 a) Sit/Stay – The Judge or Steward will direct handlers to positions in the ring. The command 'last command' will be given when all are ready and handlers should then instantly give their final command to the dogs. Any further commands or signals to the dogs after this 'last command' will be penalised. Handlers will then be instructed to leave their dogs and walk to positions indicated until ordered to return to them. Dogs should remain at the Sit position throughout the test. This is a group test and all dogs must compete together.

b) Stand/Stay – This test should be carried out exactly as for the Sit/Stay, except that dogs will be left in the Stand position throughout the Test. This is a group test and all dogs must compete together.

c) **Down/Stay** – This test should be carried out exactly as for the Sit/Stay, except that dogs will be left in the Down position throughout the Test. This is a group test and all dogs must compete together.

5 Scent Discrimination – A steward will place the scented article amongst up to a maximum of nine other articles.

In a scent test if a dog brings in a wrong article or physically fouls any article (i.e. mouths it) this article will be replaced.

The dog should at this time be facing away from the articles. On command the handler should bring the dog to a point indicated, give the dog scent and stand upright before sending the dog to find and retrieve the appropriate article. The dog should find the article and complete the test as for the Retrieve test. In all tests, scent articles are to be placed at least 2 feet apart. Limiting the time allowed for this test is at the Judge's discretion.

Class A – Handler's Scent on Handler's Article.

The judge should reject any articles he considers to be unfit by nature of their size, shape or substance and which in his opinion could have the effect of converting this elementary Scent Test into a Sight Test. In this test at least one other article must be scented by someone other than the handler and the decoy article(s) must be similar for each dog.

Class B – Handler's Scent on Article provided by the Judge.

The article must not be given to the dog. All articles must be separate and similar.

Class C – Judge's Scent on piece of marked cloth. A decoy steward should not handle a cloth for a period longer than the Judge.

Appendix 2

Kennel Club Working Trial Regulations
Reproduced by kind permission of the Kennel Club

Definition of Stakes

When entering for Championship or Open Working Trials, wins at Members Working Trials will not count.

No dog entered in P.D. or T.D. Stakes shall be eligible to enter in any other Stake at the meeting.

All Police dogs shall be considered qualified for entry in W.D. Championship Stakes if they hold the Regional Police Dog qualification 'Excellent', provided that such entries are countersigned by the Senior Police Officer I/C when such entries are made. Dogs holding this qualification are not eligible for entry in C.D. or U.D. Open or Championship Stakes, nor in W.D. Open Stakes.

No Working Trial Stake shall be limited to less than 30 dogs. If a limit is imposed on entries in any Stake, it shall be carried out by ballot after the date of closing of entries. Championship T.D. or P.D. Stakes shall not be limited by numbers in any way.

Open Working Trial

Companion Dog (C.D.) Stake. – For dogs which have not qualified C.D. Ex or U.D. Ex or won three or more first prizes in C.D. or any prize in U.D. Stakes, W.D. Stakes, P.D. or T.D. Stakes at Open or Championship Working Trials.

Utility Dog (U.D.) Stake. – For dogs which have not been awarded a Certificate of Merit in U.D., W.D., P.D. or T.D. Stakes.

Working Dog (W.D.) Stake. – For dogs which have been awarded a Certificate of Merit in U.D. Stakes but not in W.D., P.D. or T.D. Stakes.

Tracking Dog (T.D.) Stake. – For dogs which have been awarded a Certificate of Merit in W.D. Stakes but not in T.D. Stakes.

Police Dog (P.D.) Stake. – For dogs which have been awarded a Certificate of Merit in W.D. Stakes.

Championship Working Trial

Companion Dog (C.D.) Stake. – For dogs which have not won three or more first prizes in C.D. Stakes or any prize in any other Stake at Championship Working Trials.

Utility Dog (U.D.) Stake. – For dogs which have won a Certificate of Merit in an Open U.D. Stake. A dog is not eligible for entry in this Stake if it has been entered in the W.D. Stake on the same day.

Working Dog (W.D.) Stake. – For dogs which have qualified U.D. Ex and have won a Certificate of Merit in Open W.D. Stakes.

Tracking Dog (T.D.) Stake. – For dogs which have qualified W.D. Ex and have won a Certificate of Merit in Open T.D. Stakes.

Police Dog (P.D.) Stake. – For dogs which have qualified W.D. Ex.

Schedule of Exercises and Points
Companion Dog (CD) Stake

	Marks	Group Total	Minimum Group Qualifying Mark
Group I. Control			
1 Heel on Leash	5		
2 Heel Free	10		
3 Recall to Handler	5		
4 Sending the dog away	10	30	21
Group II. Stays			
5 Sit (2 Minutes)	10		
6 Down (10 Minutes)	10	20	14
Group III. Agility			
7 Scale (3) Stay (2) Recall (5)	10		
8 Clear Jump	5		
9 Long Jump	5	20	14
Group IV. Retrieving and Nosework			
10 Retrieve a dumb-bell	10		
11 Elementary Search	20	30	21
Totals	100	100	70

Utility Dog (UD) Stake

	Marks	Group Total	Minimum Group Qualifying Mark
Group I Control			
1 Heel Free	5		
2 Sending the dog away	10		
3 Retrieve a dumb-bell	5		
4 Down (10 Minutes)	10		
5 Steadiness to gunshot	5	35	25
Group II Agility			
6 Scale (3) Stay (2) Recall (5)	10		
7 Clear Jump	5		
8 Long Jump	5	20	14
Group III Nosework			
9 Search	35		
10 Track (95) Article (15)	110	145	102
Totals	200	200	141

Working Dog (WD) Stake

	Marks	Group Total	Minimum Group Qualifying Mark
Group I Control			
1 Heel Free	5		
2 Sending the dog away	10		
3 Retrieve a dumb-bell	5		
4 Down (10 Minutes)	10		
5 Steadiness to Gunshot	5	35	25
Group II Agility			
6 Scale (3) Stay (2) Recall (5)	10		
7 Clear Jump	5		
8 Long Jump	5	20	14
Group III Nosework			
9 Search	35		
10 Track (90) Articles (10 + 10 = 20)	110	145	102
Totals	200	200	141

Tracking Dog (TD) Stake

	Marks	Group Total	Minimum Group Qualifying Mark
Group I Control			
1 Heel Free	5		
2 Sendaway and Directional Control	10		
3 Speak on Command	5		
4 Down (10 Minutes)	10		
5 Steadiness to Gunshot	5	35	25
Group II Agility			
6 Scale (3) Stay (2) Recall (5)	10		
7 Clear Jump	5		
8 Long Jump	5	20	14
Group III Nosework			
9 Search	35		
10 Track (100) Articles 10 + 10 + 10 = 30)	130	165	116
Totals	220	220	155

Police Dog (PD) Stake

	Marks	Group Total	Minimum Group Qualifying Mark
Group I Control			
1 Heel Free	5		
2 Sendaway and Directional Control	10		
3 Speak on Command	5		
4 Down (10 Minutes)	10		
5 Steadiness to Gunshot	5	35	25
Group II Agility			
6 Scale (3) Stay (2) Recall (5)	10		
7 Clear Jump	5		
8 Long Jump	5	20	14
Group III Nosework			
9 Search	35		
10 Track (60) Articles (10 + 10 = 20)	80	115	80
Group IV Patrol			
11 Quartering the Ground	45		
12 Test of Courage	20		
13 Search and Escort	25		
14a Recall from Criminal	30		
14b Pursuit and Detention of Criminal	30	150	105
Totals	320	320	224

Description of Exercises and Guidance for Judges and Competitors at Working Trials

A. Method of Handling. – Although implicit obedience to all orders is necessary, dogs and handlers must operate in as free and natural a manner as possible. Excessive formalism may be penalised, particularly if, in the opinion of the Judge, it detracts from the ability of the dog to exercise its senses in relation to all that is happening in the vicinity. Persistent barking, whining, etc. in any exercise other than location of articles, person or speak on command should be penalised. Food may not be given to the dog by the handler whilst being tested.

B. Heel Work. – The Judge should test the ability of the dog to keep his shoulder reasonably close to the left knee of the handler who should walk smartly in his natural manner at normal, fast and slow paces through turns and among and around persons and obstacles. The halt, with the dog sitting to heel and a 'figure of eight' may be included at any stage.

Any act, signal or command or jerking of the leash which in the opinion of the Judge has given the dog unfair assistance shall be penalised.

C. Sit (2 Minutes). – Dogs may be tested individually or in a group or groups. The Judge or Steward will give the command 'last command' and handlers should then instantly give their final commands to the dogs. Any further commands or signals to the dogs will be penalised. Handlers will then be instructed to leave their dogs and proceed to positions indicated by the Judge or Steward until ordered to return to them. Where possible, such positions should be out of sight of the dogs but bearing in mind the short duration of the exercise this may not be practical. Dogs must remain in the sit position throughout the test until the Judge or Steward indicates that the test has finished. Minor movements must be penalised. The Judge may use his discretion should interference by another dog cause the dog to move.

D. Down (10 Minutes). – Handlers must be out of sight of the dogs who may be tested individually or in a group or groups. The Judge or Steward will give the command 'last command' and handlers should then instantly give their final commands to their dogs. Any further commands or signals to the dogs will be penalised. Handlers will then be instructed to leave their dogs and proceed to positions indicated by the Judge or Steward until ordered to return to them. Dogs must remain in the 'Down' position throughout the test until the Judge or Steward indicates that the Test has finished. No dog will be awarded any marks that sits, stands or crawls more than its approximate body length in any direction. Minor movements must be penalised. The Judge may use his discretion should interference by another dog cause a dog to move. The Judge may test the dogs by using distractions but may not call it by name.

E. Recall to Handler. – The dog should be recalled from the 'Down' or 'Sit' position. The handler being a reasonable distance from the dog at the discretion of the Judge. The dog should return at a smart pace and sit in front of the handler, afterwards going smartly to heel on command or signal. Handler to await command of the Judge or Steward.

F. Retrieve a Dumb-bell. – The dog should not move forward or retrieve nor deliver to hand on return until ordered by the handler on the Judge or Stewards' instructions. The Retrieve should be executed at a smart pace without mouthing or playing with the object. After delivery the handler will send his dog to heel on the instructions of the Judge or Steward.

G. Send Away and Directional Control. – The minimum distance that the Judge shall set for the Send Away shall be 20 yards for the CD Stake and 50 yards for all other Stakes. The TD and PD Stakes shall also include a redirection of a minimum of 50 yards. When the dog has reached the designated point or the Judge is satisfied that after a reasonable time the handler cannot improve the position of the dog by any further command the dog should be stopped in either the stand, sit or down position at the discretion of the handler. At this point in the TD or PD Stakes the Judge or Steward shall instruct the handler to redirect his dog. In all Stakes, whilst the Judge should take into account the number of commands used during the exercise, importance should be placed upon the handler's ability to direct his dog to the place indicated.

H. Steadiness to Gunshot. – The most appropriate occasion of testing this exercise would be in open country. The dog may be either walking at heel free or be away from the handler who must be permitted to remain within controlling distance whilst the gun is fired. Any sign of fear, aggressiveness or barking must be penalised. This test shall not be carried out without prior warning, or incorporated in any other test. The Judge will not provoke excitement by excessive display of the gun, nor shall the gun be pointed at the dog.

I. Speak on Command. – The Judge will control the position of the handler in relation to the dog and may require the handler to work the dog walking at heel. If the dog is not required to walk at heel, the handler may at his discretion place the dog in the stand, sit or down. The dog will be ordered to speak and cease speaking on command of the Judge or Steward who may then instruct the handler to make the dog speak again. Speaking should be sustained by the dog whilst required with the minimum of commands and/or signals. Continuous and/or excessive incitements to speak shall be severely penalised. This test should not be incorporated with any other test.

J. Agility. – No part of the scale or clear or long jump equipment to be traversed by a dog shall be less than three feet wide nor be in any way injurious to the dog. The tests shall be followed in a sequence agreed by the Judge and will commence with the Scale. The Scale should be a vertical wall of wooden planks and may have affixed on both sides three slats evenly distributed in the top half of the jump. The top surface of the Scale may be lightly padded. The handler should approach the Scale at a walking pace and halt four to nine feet in front of it and in his own time order the dog to scale. On reaching the other side the dog should be ordered to stay in the stand, sit or down position, the handler having previously nominated such a position to the Judge. The Judge should ensure that the dog will stay steady and may indicate to the handler where he should stand in relation to his dog and the Scale before ordering the dog to be recalled over the Scale. A dog which fails to go over the Scale at the second attempt shall be excluded from the stay and recall over the Scale. Failure in the recall over the Scale does not disqualify from marks previously gained.

The handler may either approach the clear and long jumps with the dog or send it forward or stand by the jumps and call the dog up to jump. At no time should the handler proceed beyond any part of the jumps before they have been traversed by the dog. Once the dog has cleared the obstacle he should remain on the other side under control until joined by the handler. The clear jump should be so constructed that it will be obvious if the dog has exerted more than slight pressure upon it. The rigid top bar may be fixed or rest in cups and the space below may be filled in but the filling should not project above the bottom of the top bar. Appreciable pressure exerted by the dog on the clear jump shall be considered to be a failure. Casual fouling with fore or hind legs will be penalised at the discretion of the Judge. Failure or refusal at any of the three types of jumps may be followed by a second attempt and any one such failure shall be penalised by at least 50% of the marks alloted to that part of the exercise in which the dog is given a second attempt.

Jumping heights and lengths:—

Companion Dog (CD) Stake and Utility Dog (UD) Stake

 (a) **Scale**

  Dogs not exceeding 10 in. at shoulder 3 ft.
  Dogs not exceeding 15 in. at shoulder 4 ft.
  Dogs exceeding 15 in. at shoulder 6 ft.

 (b) **Clear Jump**

  Dogs not exceeding 10 in. at shoulder 1 ft 6 in.
  Dogs not exceeding 15 in. at shoulder 2 ft.
  Dogs exceeding 15 in. at shoulder 3 ft.

 (c) **Long Jump**

  Dogs not exceeding 10 in. at shoulder 4 ft.
  Dogs not exceeding 15 in. at shoulder 6 ft.
  Dogs exceeding 15 in. at shoulder 9 ft.

Working Dog (WD) Stake, Tracking Dog (TD) Stake and Police dog (PD) Stake

 (a) Scale   6 ft.

(*b*) Clear Jump   3 ft.
(*c*) Long Jump   9 ft.

K. Search. – The Companion Dog (CD) Stake Search shall contain three articles and all other Stakes shall contain four articles. In all Stakes fresh articles must be placed for each dog who must recover a minimum of two articles to qualify. As a guide the articles should be similar in size to a six inch nail or a match box, but the Judge should choose articles in relation to the nature of the ground and the Stake which he is judging. The time allotted shall be four minutes in the CD Stake and five minutes in all other Stakes. The articles should be well handled and placed by a Steward who shall foil the ground by walking in varying directions over the area. Each competitor shall have a separate piece of land.

The CD Stake search area shall be 15 yards square, all other Stakes being 25 yards square and shall be clearly defined by a marker peg at each corner. The handler may work his dog from any position outside the area, provided that he does not enter it.

In the CD Stake a maximum five marks should be allotted for each article and a maximum five marks for style and control. In all other Stakes a maximum seven marks should be allotted for each article and a maximum seven marks for style and control.

L. Track. – The track should be plotted on the ground to be used for the nosework by Stewards previous to the day of commencement of the Trials. An area of ground which has had a track laid over it must not have another track laid over it until the following day. The track shall be single line and may include turns. The articles should be in keeping with the nature of the ground. There shall be a marker left by the track layer to indicate the start of the track. In the UD Stake a second marker should be left not more than 30 yards from the start to indicate the direction of the first leg.

Unless the Judge considers the dog to have lost the track beyond recovery or has run out of the time allotted for the completion of the track a handler may recast his dog at his discretion. The Judge should not at any time indicate to the handler where he should recast his dog except in exceptional circumstances.

The track shall be approximately half a mile long and should be laid as far as possible by a stranger to the dog. The article(s) should be well scented. When the judging is in progress the track layer shall be present at the side of the Judge to indicate the exact line of the track and the position of the articles.

The UD Stake track shall be not less than half an hour old and shall include one article at the end, recovery of the article not being a requirement for qualification.

The WD and PD Stake tracks shall be not less than one and a half hours old and shall include two articles one of which must be recovered to qualify.

The TD Stake track shall be not less than three hours old and shall include three articles two of which must be recovered to qualify.

In all Stakes the last article shall indicate the end of the track. No two articles should be laid together.

A spare track additional to requirements should be laid but the opportunity to run a new track should be given only in exceptional circumstances.

The area used for Tracking is out of bounds to all competitors for practice Tracks and exercise from the time of the first track and any competitor found contravening this instruction is liable to be disqualified by the Judge and/or Stewards from participating in the Trial in accordance with the provision of Regulation No. 7(c).

The dog must be worked on a harness and tracking line.

M. Quartering the Ground. – The missing person or criminal should be protected to the minimum extent consistent with safety. He should remain motionless out of sight of the handler, but should be accessible on investigation to a dog which has winded him.

The Judge should satisfy himself that the dog has found the person and has given warning spontaneously and emphatically without being directed by the handler. Once the person has been detected and the dog has given voice, he may offer meat or other food which should be refused by the dog. If the dog ignores the food he may throw it on the ground in front of the dog. A dog which bites the person or criminal must be severely penalised.

N. Test of Courage. – This is a test of courage rather than of control. Dogs will not be heavily penalised in this test for lack of control. Handlers must be prepared to have the dog tested when on the lead by an unprotected Judge or Steward, and/or when off the lead by a protected Steward. The method of testing will be at the discretion of the Judge.

O. Search and Escort. – The criminal will be searched by the handler with the dog off the lead at the sit, stand or down. The Judge will assess whether the dog is well placed tactically and ready to defend if called to do so.

The handler will then be told to escort the prisoner(s) at least 30 yards in a certain direction, he will give at least one turn on the direction of the Judge. During the exercise the criminal will turn and attempt to overcome the handler. The dog may defend spontaneously or on command and must release the criminal at once both when he stands still or when the handler calls him off. The handler should be questioned as to his tactics in positioning the dog in both search and escort.

P. Recall from Criminal. (Exercise 14(a)). – The criminal, protected to the minimum extent consistent with safety, will be introduced to the handler whose dog will be free at heel. After an unheated conversation the criminal will run away. At a reasonable distance the handler will be ordered to send his dog. When the dog is approximately halfway between handler and the criminal he will be ordered to be recalled. The recall may be by whistle or voice. The criminal should continue running until the dog returns or closes. If the dog continues to run alongside the criminal the criminal should run a further ten or dozen paces to indicate this.

Q. Pursuit and Detention of Criminal. (Exercise 14(b)). – The criminal (a different one for choice) and handler should be introduced as above, and the dog sent forward under the same conditions. The criminal must continue to attempt to escape and, if possible, should do so through some exit or in some vehicle once the dog has had a chance to catch up with him. The dog must be regarded as having succeeded if it clearly prevents the criminal from continuing his line of flight, either by holding him by the arm, knocking him over or close circling him till he becomes giddy. If the dog fails to make a convincing attempt to detain the criminal, it shall lose any marks that it may have obtained under exercise 14(a) or alternatively, it shall not be tested on exercise 14(a) if that followed exercise 14(b).

Appendix 3

Kennel Club Regulations for Agility Tests – 1st July, 1983

1 Registered Clubs, Societies, Dog Training Clubs, Kennel Club Licensed Shows and other organisations approved by the Kennel Club may hold Agility Tests. The Kennel Club reserves the right to refuse any application for a licence.

2 Applications for permission to hold Agility Tests must be made in the form of a letter to the Secretary of the Kennel Club at least six months before the date of the proposed event. A fee of £2.87 (inclusive of VAT) must be forwarded with the application together with a schedule for the event which must contain:—

(a) The date, place and time of the event.
(b) A separate official entry form which must be an exact copy of wording of the specimen entry form issued by the Kennel Club.
(c) The amounts of entry fees and any prize money.
(d) The method by which the judge will mark the tests.
(e) The qualifications for entry in the tests scheduled.
(f) An announcement that the Tests are held Kennel Club Regulations for Agility Tests.
(g) An announcement that the organising committee reserve the right to refuse any entry.
(h) The names of the judges.

3 A dog must, at the time of the competition be registered at the Kennel Club. The Committee of the organising Club may reserve the right to refuse entry.

4 Puppies under 12 calendar months of age and bitches in season are not eligible for competition in Agility Tests.

5 If a dog competes which has been exposed to the risk of any contagious or infectious disease during the period of six weeks prior to the Agility Tests and/or if any dog shall be proved to be suffering at Agility Tests from any contagious or infectious disease, the owner thereof shall be liable to be dealt with under Kennel Club Rule 17.

6 The organising Club shall keep a list of the names of all competing dogs with awards and the names and addresses of their owners for a period of twelve months from the date of the Agility Tests.

7 A judge at an Agility Test cannot compete at that event on the same day.

8 Fraudulent or Discreditable conduct at Agility Tests to be Reported:—

The Executive of the organising Club of an Agility Test must immediately report to the Secretary of the Kennel Club any case of alleged fraudulent or discreditable conduct, any default or omission at or in connection with the Agility Test which may come under its notice, and at the same time forward to the Secretary of the Kennel Club all documents and information in connection therewith, which may be in its possession or power. Where fraudulent or discreditable conduct is alleged at an Agility Test in Scotland, the Executive of the organising club must make such report in the first instance to the Secretary of the Scottish Kennel Club.

Agility Tests are considered to be a "fun" type competition designed for spectator appeal. However, competitors are reminded that they are subject to other Kennel Club Rules & Regulations where applicable.

Schedule of Tests
Agility Tests – Courses and Obstacles
The following obstacles meet with the approval of the Committee of the Kennel Club but organisers may submit others for approval if desired. No practice is to be allowed on the course.

1 *Test Area*. The test area must measure not less than 40 yards × 30 yards and have a non-slip surface.

2 *Course*. A minimum of ten and a maximum of 18 comprise a test course.

3 *Obstacles*.
(a) *Hurdle* : Height : 2 ft 6 in maximum. Width : 4 ft 0 in minimum.
(b) *Dog Walk* : Height : 4 ft 0 in minimum, 4 ft 6 in maximum. Walk plank width : 8 in minimum, 12 in maximum. Length : 12 ft 0 in minimum, 14 ft 0 in maximum. Ramps to have anti-slip slats at intervals and to be firmly fixed to top plank.
(c) *Hoop* : Aperture diameter : 1 ft 3 in minimum. Aperture centre from ground 3 ft 0 in maximum.
(d) *Brush Fence* : Dimensions as for hurdle.
(e) *Table* : Surface : 3 ft 0 in square minimum. Height : 3 ft 0 in maximum. To be of stable construction with non-slip surface.
(f) *Collapsible Tunnel* : Diameter : 2 ft 0 in minimum, 2 ft 6 in maximum. Length : 12 ft 0 in. Circular of non-rigid material construction with entrance of rigid construction and fixed or weighted to the ground.
(g) *'A' ramp* : Length : 3 yards minimum, $3\frac{1}{2}$ yards maximum. Width : 3 ft 0 in. Height of apex from ground 6 ft 3 in. Two ramps hinged at apex. Surface of ramps slatted at intervals.

(h) *Weaving Poles :* Number 6 minimum, 12 maximum. Distance apart 2 ft 0 in maximum.

(i) *Pipe Tunnel :* Diameter: 2 ft minimum. Length: 10 ft 0 in minimum.

(j) *See-Saw :* Width: 8 in minimum, 12 in maximum. Length: 12 ft 0 in minimum, 14 ft 0 in maximum. Height of central bracket from ground, 2 ft 3 in maximum. A plank firmly mounted on central bracket.

(k) *Long-jump :* Length: 5 ft maximum. Width: 4 ft minimum. Height: 1 ft maximum.

(l) *Pause Box :* Defined area 4 ft × 4 ft.

Marking

Standard Marking
5 faults for each failure to negotiate any obstacle correctly.
Failure to correctly complete the course – disqualified.

Other marking
Any form of marking other than 'Standard' must be stated in the schedule.

Appendix 4

Table of Obedience Champions – Dogs

Name of Dog	Breed	Owner at Date of Title	Date of Qualifying	No. of Obedience Certificates won, plus Crufts Championships
RAF OF SCHONE	G.S.D.	J. Kenworthy	12 Dec. 51	5
SIEGFRIED OF JOTUNHEIM	G.S.D.	G. K. Pavitt	3 May 52	5
MASTER IAN	SHETLAND SHEEPDOG	F. W. Ratcliffe	9 Dec. 52	5
PRINCE OF BARMOUTH	G.S.D.	S. J. Pavitt	21 Mar. 53	6
BRUTUS OF ANGLEZARKE	G.S.D.	Mrs P. Wilks	25 May 53	3
HASSAN OF NAVRIG	G.S.D.	J. J. Howe	15 Aug. 53	3
ANGUS OF HERONSMOOR	G.S.D.	Mrs A. W. Montgomery	9 Sept. 53	4
DILIGENT BLACKBOY	G.S.D.	J. Coomber	1 May 54	13
GHILLE OF MOSPE	SHETLAND SHEEPDOG	F. W. Ratcliffe	3 Jul. 54	14
FRANZ OF COMBEHILL	G.S.D.	I. Heward	7 Aug. 54	3
TERRIE OF GLENVOCA (CH)	G.S.D.	G. Crook	11 Sept. 54	3
SHEPERDON SPUN GOLD	G.S.D.	Miss H. D. Homan	2 Feb. 55	1 + 1 Crufts
JUPITER OF TAVEY (CH)	DOBERMANN	F. Curnow & R. M. Montgomery	8 Jun. 55	3
RAJAH OF CYMRU	G.S.D.	W. H. G. Hughes	2 Jul. 55	5
DANKIE OF GLENVOCA (CH & IRISH CH)	G.S.D.	G. Crook	16 Jul. 55	5
TARZAN OF RAINIER	G.S.D.	Mr & Mrs McGrath	3 Dec. 55	4
DASH	BORDER COLLIE	W. H. Shackleton	10 Feb. 56	5 + 2 Crufts
VAQUEEL OF KELOWNA	G.S.D.	Miss M. J. O'Grady	26 May 56	10
SILVER DANDY	G.S.D.	A. D. Ashley	7 Aug. 56	5
THE GOON	WELSH COLLIE	A. J. Montgomery	1 Sept. 56	5
SCOT OF GILLOW	BORDER COLLIE	D. Churchman	5 Sept. 56	7
LUPO DI LOMBARDIA	G.S.D.	Mr & Mrs L. M. Wood	12 Sept. 56	4
SON OF SILVERSHAN	G.S.D.	W. J. Spencer	20 Oct. 56	12
LORD BOB	BORDER COLLIE	Mrs O. E. Tate	27 Jul. 57	3
ANTON OF EYOT	MINIATURE POODLE	Miss P. M. McCudden	28 Sept. 57	3
AMPHION OF PALERMO	G.S.D.	Mr F. Hawes	7 Feb. 58	1 + 1 Crufts
BOYD OF WELLENK	G.S.D.	W. Chadwick	10 May 58	4
COMERAGH PADDY	BORDER COLLIE	Mrs B. Langley	11 Jun. 58	23
CASTLENAU PIZZICATO	GOLDEN RETRIEVER	Mrs K. Needs	6 Feb. 59	6 + 1 Crufts
AMBROSE OF KINGSTEAD	PEM. CORGI	F. Strutt	27 Jun. 59	5
VITALIS ARISTOPHANES	G.S.D	Miss P. Mayers	11 Jul. 59	3

Table of Obedience Champions – Dogs

Name of Dog	Breed	Owner at Date of Title	Date of Qualifying	No. of Obedience Certificates won, plus Crufts Championships
RORY OF LERWICK	SHETLAND SHEEPDOG	C. D. Strachan	8 Aug. 59	4
ILIAD OF TOLHURST	G.S.D.	Mrs R. M. Davis	31 Oct. 59	7 + 1 Crufts
MICHELSON OF CHAROAN	G.S.D.	Mrs L. Dance	7 Nov. 59	9
ROY'S CHOICE OF ELMTREE	G.S.D.	W. R. Lord	21 Jun. 60	3
ORPHEUS OF COMBEHILL	G.S.D.	G. Rowland	25 Jun. 60	3
ADASTRA MATELOT	MINIATURE POODLE	Mrs E. Barff	29 Jun. 60	3
COLLIES COLLIE	CROSSBR'D	R. Iremonger	19 Nov. 60	3
BLACK CLOUD	G.S.D.	J. P. Coult	10 Feb. 61	2 + 1 Crufts
ALEX OF JANPERMAZ	G.S.D.	Mr & Mrs J. Mazur	29 Apr. 61	11
CARLO OF PERRYCROFT	G.S.D.	J. T. Hudson	17 Jun. 61	4
PATANNE	BORDER COLLIE	Mrs D. M. Sandland	24 Jun. 61	4
MASTERPIECE OF MOSPE	SHETLAND SHEEPDOG	Mr & Mrs F. W. Ratcliffe	16 Sept. 61	5
GLYNN OF RIGI	BORDER COLLIE	Miss H. D. Homan	2 Nov. 61	4 + 2 Crufts
LAUREL OF VAGORLEX	G.S.D.	G. W. Carpenter	11 Nov. 61	3
VICTOR OF BALTERRA	G.S.D.	H. Allan	19 Jun. 62	7
HOLMFLOW REBEL	G.S.D.	F. Smith	7 Aug. 62	4 + 1 Crufts
BRUNO OF MENDIN	G.S.D.	J. T. Hudson	1 Sept. 62	3
EAGER MAJOR	G.S.D. CR'SS	D. Chalkey	13 Apr. 63	3
GYPSY CHIEF	WORKING COLLIE	W. J. Spencer	17 Jul. 63	7
JHETTANUND DAYCROSS	G.S.D.	R. L. Crow	28 Sept. 63	3
BLAZE OF SEALIGHT	CROSS COLLIE	Mrs P. Bellamy	25 Apr. 64	23 + 1 Crufts
MICKLYN SHANDY	LAB/COLLIE CROSS	Mrs J. M. McMillan	18 Jul. 64	19 + 1 Crufts
RIP OF RIVERDALE	CROSS COLLIE	A. Romans	4 Aug. 64	4
FLAK OF ARDGYE	G.S.D.	S. Duncan	22 Aug. 64	5 + 1 Crufts
NICHOLAS OF ALBESDON	GOLDEN RETR'VER	A. Frost	29 Aug. 64	3
MELYN OF MONKSMEAD	BORDER COLLIE	Mrs E. M. Sterrett	7 Nov. 64	9
RICKY ROYALIST	G.S.D.	Mr & Mrs R. Edwards	5 Feb. 65	1 + 1 Crufts
SHACK	BORDER COLLIE	W. H. Shackleton	3 Apr. 65	4
MIRK OF MONKSMEAD	BORDER COLLIE	L. E. Bagshaw	29 May 65	7
APOLLO OF HAWKSWOOD	G.S.D.	R. Woodcock	28 Aug. 65	3
SHEP	BORDER COLLIE	A. J. Stone	12 Feb. 66	3
SILVERSHAN OF GUILDHALL	G.S.D.	W. J. Spencer	9 Apr. 66	4
CORDO OF PERRYCOURT	G.S.D.	J. T. Hudson	14 Jun. 66	5
GLARE OF SEALIGHT	BORDER COLLIE	Mrs P. Bellamy	20 Aug. 66	17
DIRK OF TWISTWOOD	CROSSBR'D	Mrs J. Makinson	10 Feb. 67	1 + 1 Crufts

Table of Obedience Champions – Dogs

Name of Dog	Breed	Owner at Date of Title	Date of Qualifying	No. of Obedience Certificates won, plus Crufts Championships
MEGS PRIDE	BORDER COLLIE	Mrs J. Adams	1 Jul. 67	6
BWANA OF TERONY	G.S.D.	A. D. Ashley	15 Jul. 67	3
TAM II	BORDER COLLIE	Mrs J. Faulconbridge	9 Feb. 68	2 + 1 Crufts
GRINSTEDE RANGER	G.S.D.	L. G. Atkins	4 May 68	6
OUR SHEP	SHETLAND SHEEPDOG	Mr & Mrs J. D. Harris	22 Jun. 68	7
MICKLYN WHISKEY	BORDER COLLIE	Mrs J. M. McMillan	6 Jul. 68	4
HEELAWAY BESTONE	G.S.D.	C. M. Wyant	24 Aug. 68	6
MELVILLE OF MONKSMEAD	BORDER COLLIE	Mrs M. Pearce	5 Apr. 69	4
JEWEL OF MAGNUM	WORKING COLLIE	S. G. Buley	2 May 69	7
HEELAWAY AMON	G.S.D.	Mrs K. Wells	7 Jun. 69	3
JAFF	BORDER COLLIE	F. Smith	3 Sept. 69	27 + 1 Crufts
ODIN OF KENTERRA	G.S.D.	Mr & Mrs B. Schofield	27 Sept. 69	6
GOLDEN GIFT	GOLDEN RETR'VER	J. W. Burdett	25 Apr. 70	4 + 1 Crufts
BANDINO OF ROSEAVON	G.S.D.	G. Shuttleworth	23 May 70	3
KANGA OF THE BRIDGE	WORKING COLLIE	Mrs E. N. Chivers	6 Jun. 70	8
PERRIE OF GREENFORD	WORKING COLLIE	J. Kerslake	15 Aug. 70	7
PRINCE OF FIRECAVE	G.S.D.	Mrs A. S. Merry	17 Oct. 70	9
TAM OF HURSTVIEW	BORDER COLLIE	Mrs A. Sivyer	19 Jun. 71	8
SHAR OF HOWBAR	G.S.D.	C. Stephens	27 Jun. 71	5
HEELAWAY UNIT	G.S.D.	C. M. Wyant	7 Jul. 71	12
STILLMOOR JAMIE OF HURSTVIEW	BORDER COLLIE	Miss P. Ackary	21 Aug. 71	13 + 1 Crufts
TEVIS BORDER BRETT	WORKING COLLIE	F. Hamilton	4 Feb. 72	6 + 1 Crufts
SHADOWSQUAD TEAL	G.S.D.	G. Thornally	20 May 72	3
USWORTH GOBLIN	WORKING SHEEPDOG	Mrs G. G. Shield	28 Oct. 72	6
SCHULTZ OF VALHALLA	G.S.D.	A. Wilson	18 Nov. 72	9
FLETE OF TAMERRYE	BORDER COLLIE	Mrs J. E. Naylor	25 Nov. 72	18 + 1 Crufts
BOSS OF THORNEYMOOR	BORDER COLLIE	D. C. Martin	31 Mar. 73	10
TRIM OF RIVERDALE	WORKING SHEEPDOG	T. Romans	16 Jun. 73	3
JONATHAN OF BURNTHOUSE	BORDER COLLIE	Miss D. Homan & Mrs B. Langley	23 Jun. 73	8
BLAZE AWAY OF SEALIGHT	WORKING SHEEPDOG	Mrs A. Merry	14 Jul. 73	6
PRINCE OF ORMSBY	G.S.D.	D. McDonnough	15 Sept. 73	4

Name of Dog	Breed	Owner at Date of Title	Date of Qualifying	No. of Obedience Certificates won, plus Crufts Championships
MOSS OF THORNEYMOOR	BORDER COLLIE	F. D. Herman	8 Feb. 74	2 + 1 Crufts
SABRE OF POTTERSPRIDE OF BRYNBANK	G.S.D.	Mrs J. Houston	30 Mar. 74	4
ROGUE OF SEALIGHT	BORDER COLLIE	Mrs P. Bellamy	24 May 74	10
MEADOW PRINCE	CROSSBR'D CROSS	Miss M. Stephenson	19 Jul. 74	8
BEVERLEY'S PIP	COLLIE	A. D. Ashley	9 Aug. 74	3
SEORAS OF THORNEYMOOR	BORDER COLLIE	Mrs R. Scragg	22 Mar. 75	4
ROBBIE OF HURSTVIEW	BORDER COLLIE	Mrs P. Lister	3 May 75	3
SEALIGHT ZACK	WORKING SHEEPDOG	Mrs. A. Goodger	20 Jul. 75	8
ASA OF TAMERRYE	BORDER COLLIE	Mrs H. Holmes	25 Aug. 75	21
MELYN'S TIM	BORDER COLLIE	Mrs B. Bartley	25 Oct. 75	3
TANNASG TWEED	BORDER COLLIE	Mrs J. French	13 Feb. 76	1 + 1 Crufts
HEELAWAY USHER	G.S.D.	Miss P. J. Thompson	22 May 76	5
GARNAZA STEFAN	G.S.D.	M. R. Farringdon	21 Aug. 76	13
SPRINGFARM MYTH	WORKING SHEEPDOG	Mrs B. Iggluden	12 Sept. 76	7 + 1 Crufts
STENGHARI CYCLOPS	G.S.D.	J. D. Simpson	11 Feb. 77	2 + 1 Crufts
PORTHCURNO PLAYBOY	WORKING SHEEPDOG	Mrs D. Weston	30 Apr. 77	5
TEVIS BORDER JAKE	BORDER COLLIE	A. Lumley	7 May 77	5
WAGGERLAND SIMON	WORKING SHEEPDOG	M. P. Snow	22 May 77	7
GERHARD GILO	BORDER COLLIE	Mrs S. A. Potter	3 Aug. 77	9
BOB OF COLLIEHILL	BORDER COLLIE	Mrs S. E. Young	10 Sept. 77	3
SHANVAAL DANNY OF HURSTVIEW	BORDER COLLIE	H. W. Lister	29 May 78	4
GLEANNMHOR ARKUS	WORKING SHEEPDOG	Mrs E. W. Richards	12 Aug. 78	4
PORTHCURNO PIPER	WORKING SHEEPDOG	T. W. Hannam	9 Sept. 78	4
BRIG	BORDER COLLIE	J. O'Hara	28 Jul. 79	5
JANS JAY	WORKING SHEEPDOG	P. Poole	29 Jul. 79	3
SCHATTEN SA MEDAY	G.S.D.	Mrs R. Stevenson	18 Aug. 79	3
JAY JADE	WORKING SHEEPDOG	Mr & Mrs F. Smith	27 Oct. 79	6
CREST OF MUIRSIDE	WORKING SHEEPDOG	Mrs M. McKenzie	8 Feb. 80	5 + 1 Crufts

Name of Dog	Breed	Owner at Date of Title	Date of Qualifying	No. of Obedience Certificates won, plus Crufts Championships
BEN TROOPER	WORKING SHEEPDOG	J. S. Abrams	26 May 80	4
CHALKWELL GREYWOOD DANNY	WORKING SHEEPDOG	Mr & Mrs Watts	8 Jun. 80	9
SHARROBIN DAI	WORKING SHEEPDOG	C. Stephens	5 Jul. 80	11 + 1 Crufts
ROANCLOSE JAMIE OF STILLMOOR	WORKING SHEEPDOG	Miss P. Ackery	9 Jul. 80	6
WAGGERLAND WARRIOR	WORKING SHEEPDOG	M. P. Snow	12 Jul. 80	3
PHILLRICH BEN	WORKING SHEEPDOG	M. Yates	10 Aug. 80	4
TANNASG TOBIN	BORDER COLLIE	Mrs C. E. Robson	30 Aug. 80	5
GERARD GEMMAS LAD	WORKING SHEEPDOG	H. Watson	31 May 81	8
SHEPPY SOYEZ	WORKING SHEEPDOG	Miss M. Giampaolo	29 Aug. 81	4
TRICLEN DUKE OF GREAT MEADOWS	WORKING SHEEPDOG	Mrs V. J. Knights	13 Feb. 82	1 + 1 Crufts
RAF OF BLEATARN	WORKING SHEEPDOG	Mrs. L. Dale	10 Apr. 82	3
FLINT	BORDER COLLIE	J. O'Hara	17 Apr. 82	3
TERRIBLE TODDY SONOFYUKI	WORKING SHEEPDOG	D. Walton	29 May 82	4
BILL O' THE WISP	BORDER COLLIE	P. W. Miles	29 Jun. 82	4
WIGGY LEE OF LOOVILLE	WORKING SHEEPDOG	D. Hines	4 Sept. 82	3

(Complete up to and including 1st January 1983)

Table of Obedience Champions – Bitches

Name of Dog	Breed	Owner at Date of Title	Date of Qualifying	No. of Obedience Certificates won, plus Crufts Championships
SAPPHO OF LADOGA	G.S.D.	H. Dearman	21 Apr. 51	7
ENNICE OF MOSSVILLE	G.S.D.	E. Sandon-Moss	3 Jun. 51	7
CROFTHOLME WHILEMINA	G.S.D.	E. Morgan	3 May 52	3
MERLINSVALE CRYSTAL	G.S.D.	Miss B. V. Pindar	28 Jun. 52	5
ZENA	WORKING COLLIE	W. H. Shackleton	30 Aug. 52	18 + 2 Crufts
DELLA OF GIPTON	G.S.D.	W. J. Spencer	1 Nov. 52	11 + 1 Crufts
MAGDA OF ARDAVON	G.S.D.	Mrs D. Barton	24 Jun. 53	3
JANE OF SEAL	G.S.D.	W. Fraser	4 Jul. 53	3
JOY OF QUAINTON	G.S.D.	Miss E. K. Jones	4 Nov. 53	4
AMBER SUNLIGHT	LABRADOR RETR'VER	W. R. Lord	6 Mar. 54	4
TACKLEWAY FANTASIA	G.S.D.	Major & Mrs. J. F. H. Clare	14 Jul. 54	3
WANDA OF TANKERSLEY	LABRADOR RETR'VER	Miss U. M. Ogle	23 Apr. 55	3
ARIEL OF SWANSFORD	G.S.D.	Wing Cdr. J. Connell	22 Jun. 55	4
HONOUR BRIGHT OF SURREYHILLS	SHETLAND SHEEPDOG	Mrs C. C. Glasse	3 Sept. 55	3
YELRUTH ANNFIELD	SHETLAND SHEEPDOG	Mrs M. Pearce	14 Sept. 55	5
AMARYLLIS OF HELMDON (W.T.CH)	G.S.D.	Mrs D. Foreman	11 Feb. 56	17 + 1 Crufts
BELLE OF KILMAURS	G.S.D.	M. Porterfield	25 Feb. 56	4
GREYVALLEY CHLOE	G.S.D.	Miss B. V. Pindar	7 Apr. 56	3
LASSIE OF VENROM	G.S.D.	J. Moir Jnr.	18 Aug. 56	4
COMERAGH MUFFIN	BORDER COLLIE	Mrs. B. Langley	31 Oct. 56	3
COPYRIGHT OF ROZAVEL	G.S.D.	Mrs V. M. Jones	9 Feb. 57	2 + 1 Crufts
VICKI OF KNOCKINDU	G.S.D.	Mrs V. Rickett	23 Feb. 57	3
STORMY SUSANNAH	G.S.D.	Mrs P. Reader-Harris	22 Jun. 57	3
DELLA OF GLENVOCA	G.S.D.	W. Chappell	13 Jul. 57	3
SOUTHDOWN CASPIA (W.T.CH)	G.S.D.	Mrs D. Foreman	27 Jul. 57	7
MEGAN OF MONKSMEAD	BORDER COLLIE	Mrs M. Pearce	6 Aug. 57	52 + 4 Crufts
RAFINA OF SCHONE	G.S.D.	Mr & Mrs W. S. Randall	12 Oct. 57	10 + 1 Crufts
ISOBELLE OF ROZAVEL	G.S.D.	Miss U. Ogle	11 Jun. 58	3
SAFETY FIRST FROM SHIEL	SHETLAND SHEEPDOG	Mrs J. M. McMillan	19 Jul. 58	4
CHRISTEL OF LLANYRAVON	G.S.D.	W. J. Spencer	8 Nov. 58	4
GLENVOCA CURRACLOE GRANIA	G.S.D.	H. Blom	21 Feb. 59	3
ROSEMARY OF OCKENDEN	G.S.D.	H. Taylor	27 Jun. 59	11
AMANDA OF JUMARAL	G.S.D.	Miss J. Bate	25 Jul. 59	5 + 1 Crufts
JENNY OF RIGI	BORDER COLLIE	Miss H. D. Homan	31 Oct. 59	3
CHICO	WELSH COLLIE	Miss M. Williams	7 May 60	3

Table of Obedience Champions – Bitches

Name of Dog	Breed	Owner at Date of Title	Date of Qualifying	No. of Obedience Certificates won, plus Crufts Championships
DAWNWAY BUSY BEE	PEM.WELSH CORGI	A. E. Hutchinson	22 Jun. 60	5
GREYVALLEY FRANZI	G.S.D.	Miss B. V. Pindar	29 Jun. 60	22
SEA HOLLY	G.S.D.	Mrs N. Hills	14 Sept. 60	4
SHEBA OF DALE	G.S.D.	Mr & Mrs A. F. Sowter	7 Aug. 61	3
TESSA'S MEG	CROSSBR'D	Miss N. Adams	13 Dec. 61	5
BLACK DIAMOND OF BOTHKENNAR	SHETLAND SHEEPDOG	Miss J. Sharpe	23 Jun. 62	3
BROCKENHEIM JESS	BORDER COLLIE	G. Rockcliffe	15 Dec. 62	5
LADY OF BRUDERKERN	G.S.D.	Miss P. Core	27 Mar. 63	13
CAROLINE OF HANKLEY	G.S.D.	C. M. Wyant	4 May 63	13
FERN OF GREYVALLEY	BORDER COLLIE	Miss B. V. Pindar	8 Jun. 63	3
BRIGHT FUTURE	G.S.D.	Mr & Mrs W. Highcock	12 Jun. 63	3
GYPSY QUEEN	WORKING COLLIE	W. J. Spencer	13 Jul. 63	3
ANIELA OF JANPERMAZ	G.S.D.	R. G. Hill	16 Nov. 63	8
TURO OF EURONY	G.S.D.	J. K. Ward	2 May 64	3
VALERIE OF CREMAS	G.S.D.	Mrs R. M. Davis	23 May 64	5
ENJAKES KIM	G.S.D.	N. Stephens	8 Jul. 64	6
HANKLEY ANDROMEDA (W.T.CH)	G.S.D.	Mrs D. Foreman	6 Feb. 65	2 + 1 Crufts
BALLERINA OF HANKLEY (W.T.CH)	G.S.D.	Mrs D. Foreman	7 Aug. 65	5
JILL OF BROSTER	G.S.D.	J. Brough	28 Aug. 65	3
BENHOOKS ZENA	G.S.D.	Mrs B. Crumpton	4 Sept. 65	3
CANDY CARRIAD	BORDER COLLIE	Mrs P. Dalton	2 Oct. 65	4
SHE'S TIFFIN	SHEEPDOG	Mrs J. M. Warren	21 May 66	3 + 1 Crufts
HALAN JILL (W.T.CH)	G.S.D.	H. Allan	15 Oct. 66	6
SEAANCA FERN	BORDER COLLIE	Mrs M. E. Mulvany	6 May 67	14
CALLAG	BORDER COLLIE	Mrs F. H. Holmes	20 May 67	3
JANIE OF HAWGROVE	G.S.D.	J. Gonzales	3 Jun. 67	3
MOSS	BORDER COLLIE	Miss A. Cuddihy	1 Jul. 67	6 + 1 Crufts
BET	BORDER COLLIE	J. Seal	15 Jul. 67	34
TRUDIE OF HYTHEFIELD	G.S.D.	W. Sivyer	11 Sept. 67	3
KELPIE OF THE BRIDGE	WORKING COLLIE	Mrs E. N. Chivers	14 Oct. 67	6
INGE SHAH OF WESTONVALE	G.S.D.	J. Reeve	10 Feb. 68	6 + 1 Crufts
CORRAN LEA	BORDER COLLIE	Mrs J. Makinson	11 Jun. 68	6
HAZEL	BORDER COLLIE	Miss D. Thear	31 May 69	4
SCAPA	BEARDED COLLIE	Miss J. Cooke	6 Sept. 69	3

Table of Obedience Champions – Bitches

Name of Dog	Breed	Owner at Date of Title	Date of Qualifying	No. of Obedience Certificates won, plus Crufts Championships
LASSIE'S PRIDE	CROSSBR'D	Miss D. Terry	11 Oct. 69	3
MERRYE	BORDER COLLIE	Mrs H. Holmes	7 Feb. 70	13 + 2 Crufts
TALA	BORDER COLLIE	Mrs A. Bryce	9 May 70	3
NANA OF BOURNEMOUTH	GOLDEN RETR'VER	R. J. Knight	16 May 70	3
BLONDEL OF JAKALEDE	G.S.D.	H. W. Lister	6 Jun. 70	17
LOWENBOURNES KRYSTAL OF GREYVALLEY	G.S.D.	Mrs B. V. Hill	20 Jun. 70	12
PRIDE OF ASKHAM	MINIATURE POODLE	J. O'Hara	19 Sept. 70	4
SHEPDINE BONNIE OF SEALIGHT	WORKING COLLIE	B. G. Jordan	6 Feb. 71	9 + 1 Crufts
GLEE OF SEALIGHT	BORDER COLLIE	Mrs E. M. McCrae	24 Apr. 71	8
KENBELLAS JOODY	G.S.D.	K. G. Barley	22 May 71	6
DERRICKS DELIGHT	WORKING COLLIE	Mr & Mrs R. Wathall	3 Jul. 71	8
LOWENBOURNES FAWN	BORDER COLLIE	Mrs B. Browning	7 Jul. 71	3
LOWENBOURNES GWEN	BORDER COLLIE	Mrs D. M. Sandland	24 Jul. 71	3
RHODORA FREEDA OF SEALIGHT	BORDER COLLIE	Mrs P. Bellamy	2 Oct. 71	4
KIKKI AV FOSS	G.S.D.	A. D. Collins	16 Oct. 71	3
KINDERSYDE RAVEN	G.S.D.	Mrs B. Collins	5 Feb. 72	1 + 1 Crufts
RANVIC GERDA	G.S.D.	Mrs. J. Randall	30 May 72	4
MORWENNA OF MONKSMEAD	BORDER COLLIE	Mrs M. Pearce	22 Jun. 72	4
GREYVALLEY HONEY	G.S.D.	Mrs B. V. Hill	19 Aug. 72	17 + 1 Crufts
DAINTREE DEBUTANTE OF HALLOMAS	G.S.D.	Mrs S. A. Snook	23 Sept. 72	6 + 1 Crufts
SPRINGFARM QUIVER	WORKING SHEEPDOG	Mrs E. S. Johnson	12 Jan. 73	3
TEVIS VICTORIA	WORKING COLLIE	Mrs E. Armstrong	26 May 73	4
HEELAWAY CORA OF HANKLEY	G.S.D.	C. M. Wyant	23 Jun. 73	3
GLITTER OF SEALIGHT	BORDER COLLIE	Mrs. J. Randall	25 Aug. 73	7
JAN OF STRAD	BORDER COLLIE	Mrs W. Pykett	27 Aug. 73	11
MEIKLESTONE MOONDUST	G.S.D.	L. Telford	13 Oct. 73	9
MISCHIEF OF TAMERRYE	BORDER COLLIE	Miss I. Standfield	9 Feb. 74	7 + 1 Crufts
MEG	BORDER COLLIE	T. Romans	2 Aug. 74	4
ENCHANTED BLUE STAR	WORKING SHEEPDOG	Mrs S. A. Bishop	19 Apr. 75	24

Name of Dog	Breed	Owner at Date of Title	Date of Qualifying	No. of Obedience Certificates won, plus Crufts Championships
TEVIS BORDER LASS	BORDER COLLIE	Miss N. Jude	24 May 75	6
MOLLY OF HURSTVIEW	WORKING SHEEPDOG	Mrs V. M. Jones	4 June 75	3
LOUVILLE TANZY	WORKING SHEEPDOG	Mrs M. Howell	12 Jul. 75	7 + 1 Crufts
KATHMICK SARA	WORKING COLLIE	D. Purcell	6 Aug. 75	6
WOODSIDE SHELLEY	WORKING SHEEPDOG	S. Hollidge	9 Aug. 75	4
TANA OF WRAYSBURY	G.S.D.	R. Willet	7 Sept. 75	3
SPRINGFARM LACEY	WORKING SHEEPDOG	Mrs E. S. Johnson	11 Apr. 76	5
SHANVAAL FLURRY	BORDER COLLIE	Mrs. O. Smith	1 May 76	5
TEVIS BORDER BLITZ	BORDER COLLIE	T. R. Hall	31 May 76	5
CHADSALL TWIG	BORDER COLLIE	C. Briggs	4 Sept. 76	10
FARMERS JESS	BORDER COLLIE	Mrs R. M. Skeates	8 Jan. 77	3
MOORLAND DONNA	WORKING COLLIE	Miss A. I. Whittaker	11 Apr. 77	3
GINTHERSUN AMBER	G.S.D.	Mrs J. D. Miller	7 May 77	3
SHEPDINE BRIAR	WORKING SHEEPDOG	A. Hunt	10 Sept. 77	8
SHANVAAL BIBA	BORDER COLLIE	Miss K. Faiers	11 Sept. 77	12
SHANVAAL FLYCKA	BORDER COLLIE	J. R. Smith	17 Sept. 77	8
LOWELLA OF GREAT MEADOWS (W.T.CH)	WORKING SHEEPDOG	Mrs K. A. Smith	12 Feb. 78	13 + 2 Crufts
DEBBIE	BORDER COLLIE	Mrs V. Hall	29 May 78	4
POLZACK PURDEY OF KENSTAFF	WORKING SHEEPDOG	Miss E. Andrews	1 Jul. 78	20
KENTYGERN KATIE	WORKING SHEEPDOG	Mrs G. English	2 Sept. 78	9
CINDY FROM FROBISHER	WORKING SHEEPDOG	Miss J. A. Herring	9 Feb. 79	14 + 2 Crufts
SEALIGHT PENNY	BORDER COLLIE	Mrs P. Bellomy	18 Aug. 79	3
YVO YVONNE	G.S.D.	Mrs G. White	27 Oct. 79	16
SEALIGHT ZELAH	WORKING SHEEPDOG	Mrs E. M. Turkentine	26 Apr. 80	4
SEALIGHT DUST	WORKING SHEEPDOG	D. V. Carver	9 Aug. 80	3
RINTILLOCH GINGHA	G.S.D.	Miss K. M. Russell	13 Sept. 80	4 + 1 Crufts
SADGHYL BECK	WORKING SHEEPDOG	K. D. Forge	11 Oct. 80	3

Name of Dog	Breed	Owner at Date of Title	Date of Qualifying	No. of Obedience Certificates won, plus Crufts Championships
PRINCE SAMS JUDY	BORDER COLLIE	J. McPride	6 Jun. 81	3
BESS OF KENSTAFF	BORDER COLLIE	Mrs B. Clarke	5 Jul. 81	3
TRICLEN ECHO OF GREAT MEADOWS	WORKING SHEEPDOG	Mrs P. Beeton	5 Aug. 81	6
RODHILL FROSTED CHERRY	SHETLAND SHEEPDOG	Miss J. H. Riley	16 Aug. 81	6
WAGGERLAND WITCHCRAFT	WORKING SHEEPDOG	Mrs B. Iggulden	12 Sept. 81	3
CHALKWELL VIKKI	WORKING SHEEPDOG	Mr &Mrs R. Alleborne	10 Apr. 82	5
MIST	BORDER COLLIE	E. Quirk	13 Jun. 82	3
KENTYGERN KATASTROPHIE	WORKING SHEEPDOG	Mrs J. English	26 Jun. 82	3

(Complete up to and including 1st January 1983)

Index

road safety 39–40
road work 90
routine 22, 36

scent:
  importance of 17–18, 96
  Class A 98
  Class B 102
  Class C 102–3
Search 106
see-saw 94
Sendaway 83–9, *86*
senses:
  domination of dogs'
    behaviour by 16
  hearing 18
  scent 17–18
  sight 17

sixth sense 18–19
  taste 19
Sit:
  adult 61, *78*
  puppy 39, 78
snacks 21
socialising 36
Speak on command 110
Stand 75–6, 77
Stays, 75–80, *80*

Taste 19
Terriers 34
timing 55
titbits 16, 51
touch 19
Toy Dogs 34
Tracking 109–10

training clubs 46, 55
travelling 36–7

Utility Group 33

ventilation 26–7
veterinary advice 26
vibration, dogs' sensing of 19
vision 17
voice control 13–14, 61

Weaving poles 95
wind direction (in scenting)
  106–7, *107*
women and dogs 22
Working Group 33
Working Trials (K.C.)
  Appendix 2